I0049240

# BEYOND 401(K)

## Retirement Security in an Insecure World

**Dennis Noss MPH, MSc., Enrolled Agent**

IRS Enrolled Agent

with Edward A. Lyon, JD

Cayman Capital Management, Inc.

Registered Investment Advisor

https://CCMWealthStrategies.com

Copyright © 2025 by Captain Loopholes, LLC

All rights reserved. No part of this book may be reproduced or transmitted in any form or by any means without written permission from the author.

Library of Congress Control Number: 2025920188

ISBN: 979-8-9929944-6-9

Published by: Revision Publishing LLC

Printed In United States of America

**Other books by Dennis Noss, MSc., E.A. and Edward A. Lyon, JD**

*How to Beat the IRS, Legally*

# Introduction

This book is an understandable investigative analysis and fact finding like the "what, when, where, and how" science practiced by an epidemiology public health researcher. This easy to-follow book discloses proven plans of action that have been updated for the "what, when, where, and how" that are essential for achieving optimal financial health for your retirement wealth. Epidemiology is the branch of medical science that investigates all the factors that determine diseases and disorders that can affect the required prolonged health of our society and our economy. Alicia Munnell and Annia Sudden in their book "Coming Up Short" The Challenge of 401(k) plans makes the argument that there are still many unresolved persistent maladies that cause our aging population to not have the safety needed for accumulating an adequate greater retirement income needed for a population that is now living longer because of better healthcare and healthy living.

The overall defining characteristic of 401(k) plans is that retirement savings both enjoy the gains and suffer the losses of their investments. During the first Trump

Administration the uncertainty of risk presented a catastrophic loss for the State of California Pension Plans CallPERS and CalSTERS. These pension plans still have not fully recovered from the loss of billions of dollars in the stock market continuing to affect the retirement lifestyles of over one million State employees. This book will present new insights and better ways to prevent running out of money with your 401(k). This book answers the "what, when, where, and how" for successful management of accumulating more retirement money without having a joint account with the IRS as your surviving partner and partner for life. The traditional infrastructure of the present retirement system was created by the government, serves the government, works better for the government, and was secondarily made to also work for you with shortcomings that are your problem. Effective prudent strategic tax planning alternatives have not been given adequate public attention or have been maligned by wrong perceptions or the right solution not properly being designed by the right professional.

There are many different good strategy choices to accomplish this undertaking as no one size fits all. The best choice my tax professor used to say the answer is "it depends." You can deduct or not pay tax on income or profits and on almost anything with the right advice.

However, this book will introduce a choice that is one of the safest and better directions known and used by tax and estate planning attorneys when considering their clients' best interests. You will discover how you can save, protect and maximize your retirement money, without the IRS in your wallet. If you want to fire the IRS and keep more of the money you worked to save for yourself and your family, or leave to your children or a charity, this is the book that will tell you how to take the higher road. If you ever read the classic book by M. Scott Peck, M.D. "The Road Less Traveled" this is" The Road Less Traveled" for your "Retirement". The advice in this book is the higher road I am advocating you take, as an opportunity for a higher future income, keeping more of your retirement savings, and knowing you will have the money you will need, to maintain a better quality of life in the future and for those unexpected expensive emergencies.

# About the Author

**Dennis Noss,** MSc. IRS Enrolled Agent

Dennis Noss has a Master's of Science in Finance and Accounting from the University of Leicester in England and Master of Public Health from Loma Linda University in California where he studied epidemiology.

(Dr.) Dennis Noss is licensed and practiced as a podiatric physician and surgeon. He decided on a full-time career as a tax strategist and registered financial advisor when he was offered the opportunity to take over his family's financial advisory business more than 20 years ago.

Dennis Noss is CEO of his own firm as a Retirement and Tax Strategist and is a securities licensed registered investment advisor. He became certified professionally in retirement planning and in taxation as he feels the biggest threat to his client's future income has been inflation and taxation.

Dennis Noss specializes in custom built tax-efficient asset and stock market portfolios with more safety, less volatility, have less expenses, can minimize and protect against loss, have higher rates of return and can amplify returns for maximized income, but also minimize or eliminate the tax.

Dennis Noss is a long-standing and current investment professional member of CFA Institute and has now been active in the financial industry for more than 20 years.

Dennis Noss is regulated as a fiduciary by the Department of Financial Oversight. As a fiduciary, it is his responsibility to strive to achieve the best results for his clients.

Dennis Noss is also federally licensed as an Enrolled Agent by the Department of the Treasury, with unlimited rights to practice before the IRS concerning all tax matters, including retirement plan actions, appeals and mediation.

Dennis Noss limits his tax practice to representation, individual and business tax planning, asset and investment tax planning strategies, and integrating financial services when appropriate. He does not do tax returns for clients and will refer you to a CPA or tax attorney if needed.

Dennis Noss is a past president of the IRS Enrolled Agent Society in San Jose, California. The license to practice as an Enrolled Agent is the highest credential issued by the Department of the Treasury to the IRS for competence in federal taxation. Some CPAs and attorneys also have this designation. Very few investment advisors also have this designation.

# About the Co-Author

## Edward A. Lyon, JD

Edward Lyon, JD, earned his bachelor's degree from Hamilton College and his JD from the University of Cincinnati College of Law, where he served as Executive Editor of the University of Cincinnati Law Review.

Edward Lyon, JD, has nearly three decades of experience in the tax and financial services industries, where he focuses on helping business owners take advantage of the tax code's legal "green lights" to pay less. He's the founder and CEO of the Tax Master Network, where he created the Tax Architect software program and helped train over 4,000 tax professionals across the country. Edward is currently the Chief Tax Planner for Excel Empire, where he created the Certified Tax and Business Advisor program.

Edward is also the author of nearly a dozen books on taxes and tax planning. He writes two weekly tax columns for over 100,000 tax professionals and their clients, making him the most widely read tax strategist in the country. He's appeared on over 500 television and radio broadcasts, including CNN, Fox News, MSNBC, and CNBC.

# Table of Contents

Introduction                                                    5

About the Author                                                8

About the Co-Author                                            11

## Chapter One: The Plan                                       15

## Chapter Two: Problems with The Plan                         27

Headwind #1: Market Risk                                       30

Headwind #2: Tax Risk                                          37

Headwind #3: Contribution Limits                              49

Headwind #4: Required Minimum Distributions                   51

Headwind #5: Business Owners' Dilemma                         54

Headwind #6: Losing Your Legacy                               57

## Chapter Three: Alternatives to The Plan                    59

Roth Accounts                                                 61

Taxable Brokerage Accounts                                   63

   Cash                                        63

   Bonds                                       63

   Stocks                                      64

   Mutual Funds                                65

Real Estate                                                  67

Cash Value Life Insurance                                    71

## Chapter Four: The "Beyond 401(k)" Solution      75

*How IUL Works*      81

*Crediting Method*      86

    *Participation Rate*      87

    *Threshold Rate*      87

    *Cap Rate*      88

*How IUL Manages Volatility*      90

*How IUL Manages Taxes*      92

*IUL Premiums Versus 401(k) Contributions*      102

*IUL for Business Owners*      104

## Chapter Five: More IUL Opportunities      107

*The Death BeneXit*      107

*Family Bank*      109

*Premium*      118

*The 401(k)-to-IUL Conversion*      120

*The IUL-Financed Roth Conversion*      122

## Chapter Six: Two Objections, Answered      125

*Should I "Buy Term and Invest the Difference"?*      125

*Conclusion: Wrapping It All Up*      134

# The plan

What does the word "retirement" mean to you? Endless games of golf or pickleball in the bright Florida sun? Volunteering in your local community? Getting big in the grandchild business? Continuing your career in an "of counsel"-type role? Whatever your answer might be, it probably doesn't include "working because you have to" or "living on Social Security." And that means working to save enough to generate the income you'll need for financial independence, however you define it.

Considering how much most Americans think about retirement, and plan for it, and dream of it, and anticipate it, it's sometimes hard to realize what a new phase of life retirement is. It wasn't too long ago that most Americans worked right up until they died. Or, if they were lucky, they took good care of their kids until sending them off to work in the coal mine or bobbin factory at age 8, and hoped the kids would return the favor for a couple of years at the end of their life.

Today, most experts liken retirement planning to a three-legged stool. Those legs include pensions, Social Security, and private savings. But less than one-third of retirees—mostly those who worked for federal, state, or local governments— receive any sort of pension. And the average Social Security benefit, as of January 2023, was just $1,691.53 per month. That means you're mostly on your own when it comes to paying for all that golf and all those grandchildren. Is it any wonder that some experts have added a fourth stool—some form of continued employment—to the mix?

How are you going to finance your golden years? How much will you need? How will you grow that nest egg? How will you manage it once you start withdrawing from it so that it will last you the rest of your life?

They say a picture is worth a thousand words. So let me condense the entire challenge of today's retirement into a single image.

## Accumulation          Withdrawal

How *Much* Can You Save?

How Fast Will it Grow?

How *Long* Can You Save?

How Much Per Withdrawal?

How Fast Will It Still Grow?

How Long Will it Have to Last?

Financing retirement through a 401(k) typically consists of two phases. First, there's an accumulation phase, which is when you build your nest egg. Financial planners often recommend shooting to provide 80% of your pre retirement income. And second, there's a distribution phase when you start consuming that egg—and hopefully don't run out!

Your accumulation phase turns on three primary questions:

1. How much can you stash in your account every paycheck (or month or year)?
2. How fast will your savings grow?
3. How much time do you have to grow your portfolio?

How much can you stash in your account every paycheck (or month or year)? What sort of one-time dump-ins will you be able to add from inheritances or selling a business or investment property? This phase is hard, since saving money for retirement means not spending those same dollars on current consumption. Most experts recommend saving 10% of your gross income as soon as that becomes financially feasible. Most employers will help with some sort of matching or profit-share contributions—the national average is around 3.5%.

How fast will your savings grow? This is primarily a function of asset allocation—the strategic choices you make between stocks and other equity investments, bonds and other fixed income investments, and cash.

Will you be aggressive and shoot to beat "the market," or at least match it? Or are you uncomfortable with market volatility and better suited to a more conservative portfolio?

How much time do you have to grow your portfolio? If you start young, you'll find yourself in better shape as retirement draws near. Albert Einstein called compound interest the eighth wonder of the world. But it takes time to harvest compound interest's rewards.

Oh, and you have to do it all while you're meeting more immediate financial goals! Paying off student loans. Buying a house. Raising your children. (The US Department of Agriculture estimates it costs between $15,438 and $17,375 per year to raise a child.) Sending those kids to college. It's all too easy to put off saving for retirement while you meet those needs.

The answers to those questions determine your final nest egg. And if you fall short in one area, you can possibly make up the difference in the other two. If you're young and you can't realistically save 10%, that by itself doesn't mean you can't still succeed. You'll just need to contribute more or earn a higher return as you continue to grow. If you're not comfortable investing aggressively, you can contribute more or retire later. And if you didn't start saving until 40, you can still succeed if you save enough and grow enough between now and your eventual finish line.

At some point, you'll retire and reverse those efforts.

Don't underestimate how hard that can be! Getting rich and staying rich are two very different challenges. The world is littered with the carcasses of high-flyers who shot to the top of various "rich lists," only to lose it all because they prioritized short-term growth over long-term sustainability, often fueled by excessive leverage and unsustainable lifestyles.

How fast will you take money out? There's an entire academic discipline dedicated to answering that question. Conventional wisdom says you can take 4% per year and be reasonably sure you'll never run out of money. But that 4% papers over a lot of subtleties. And in fact, most retirees wind up taking far less than they could afford. While that leaves them financially secure, it comes at the cost of unnecessary worry. In the end, their heirs get a windfall that Mom and Dad could have used for a more comfortable time of their own.

What sort of return will you earn on your account as you start withdrawals rather than contributions? Most investors will shift at least some of their assets out of equities and into fixed income as they get older. However, many get too cautious as they age, and they fail to take advantage of guaranteed investment and income sources that can mitigate that challenge.

How long will your money have to last? This question confronts the risk of outliving your money. If you work until you're 80 and you smoke two packs a day, you're less likely to run out of money than if you retire at 65 and spend an hour on the Peloton Bike every day. Why? Because you'll die sooner, that's why! Either way, most retirees have a genuine fear of outliving their money. And it's a legitimate fear—if you've ever seen someone slowly (or suddenly) realize they're about to hit that wall, it's not a pretty sight!

If you're like most affluent Americans, you'll tackle the challenge we just pictured through an employer-sponsored, defined contribution, self directed retirement plan. That means a SIMPLE IRA or 401(k) if you work in the private sector, a 403(b) plan if you work in education or the nonprofit sector, or a 457 plan if you work for the government. This book uses the term "401(k)" for simplicity's sake. However, the problems and solutions we present generally apply to all of them. The rest of this book walks through some of the flaws challenging that model and gives you a specific solution that I would be delighted to help you implement.

The Revenue Act of 1978 first gave Americans the option of "deferring" compensation from bonuses or stock options into a profit-sharing plan. In 1981, the IRS issued rules allowing them to defer regular salaries, too. By 1996, 401(k) balances had grown to a trillion dollars. Today, 60 million Americans participate, and collectively they hold $4.8 trillion in their plan accounts.

Early backers weren't looking to start a revolution. They just wanted to give employees a way to supplement their company pension plans. Gerald Facciani, the former head of the American Society of Pension Actuaries, told the Wall Street Journal: "The great lie is that the 401(k) was capable of replacing the old system of pensions," and "it was oversold." Ted Benna, a benefits consultant who's been called "the father of the 401(k)," says it gives savers too many chances to make mistakes and "helped open the door for too many chances to make mistakes and "helped open the door for Wall Street to make even more money than they were already making Wall Street to make even more money than they were already making."

Nevertheless, corporate America couldn't resist the temptation to dump the burden of saving for retirement onto their employees' laps. Today, if you're concerned enough to save for your future retirement, it probably looks something like this:

You "defer" part of every paycheck into your account.

Your employer may (or may not) match part of your contribution, up to a set percentage of your income. Alternatively, they may (or may not) make a profit-sharing contribution—again, up to a percentage of your salary. Most employers match contributions in cash. However, some employers make matching or profit-share contributions with company stock. Those contributions may become yours immediately, or there may be a "vesting" schedule.

You choose investments from a menu of options—typically, mutual funds. Some smaller plans offer funds from just one family or group variable annuity contract. Others offer an all-you can-eat buffet of choices. The Investment Company Institute, a mutual fund trade group, reports that the average plan offers around 25 choices, including money market or FDIC insured savings accounts, short-term and long term bond funds, and large-cap and small-cap domestic and international stock funds. Some plans offer "target-date" funds designed to take the guesswork out of allocating assets yourself. Some plans even offer a "brokerage window" that lets you buy and sell individual stocks.

You watch your account grow (or shrink) over time. You can move money from one fund to another, usually at any time you like. There's no tax on interest or dividends you earn in your account. And there's no tax on gains you earn when you switch from one option to another.

If you need money from your plan, you may or may not be allowed to take a loan (nontaxable) or hardship distribution (taxable). Any distribution before age 59½ is subject to an extra 10% penalty tax.

When you switch jobs, you may or may not be allowed to keep your money with your old employer. Or you can roll it to your new employer or your own individual retirement account (IRA).

When you retire, you'll typically roll your account into your own IRA to take advantage of more investment choices than you had with your employer's plan. That's when a new challenge starts – balancing the demands of continuing to grow the account while you start drawing it down to replace the salary you just lost.

It's a great concept, at least in theory. Start saving 10% of your pretax salary as soon as you get out of college. Aim to save eight times your annual salary by the time you retire, and you'll be all good. Of course, lots of things that look great in theory fall apart in the cold clear light of day. So now, let's look at how it all works in the real world.

# Problems with The Plan

Everyone has a plan until they get punched in the mouth.

Mike Tyson

That's the plan. Really, that's all it takes. Save diligently, invest intelligently, and give yourself the time you need to grow your nest egg. Then spend responsibly, balance your need for long term portfolio growth against your need to avoid short-term downdrafts, and enjoy financial security to 100.

So, how's that working out for everyone?

Well, according to the U.S. Census Bureau, the average retirement income for individuals aged 65 and older is $75,254. The average Social Security benefit is $21,924. That means if we use the 4% rule as a guideline, the average retiree needs $1,333,250 at retirement to make up the difference.

If you're earning more than the average today in your working years, and you want to maintain your above-average lifestyle after you retire, you'll need a bigger nest egg. If you're earning significantly more than average now, and you want to maintain your significantly above-average lifestyle, you'll need even more than that.

You'll also need to consider the overall trajectory of your retirement years. Most people who retire— especially those who retire early— have a whole life left to live:

Those first few years of retirement are sometimes called the "go-go" years. They're full of travel, golf, winters down south (or relocation), and other adventures. Those take money, meaning you might even spend more than you did in your final, sprint-to-the-finish working years. It's not uncommon for people who expect to spend less in retirement than they spent while working to find themselves spending more. Those years will be even more expensive if you have to cover your own healthcare costs before Medicare kicks in!

The next few years, as you get older, are sometimes called the "go-slow" years. You'll still be traveling, but you'll be traveling to see the grandchildren, not climb Machu Picchu. You'll still be playing golf, but you'll be playing fewer rounds, and your joints will be stiffer when you step off the course.

The final phase of retirement, which can last a decade or more, is sometimes called the "no-go" years. Life in your eighties and nineties can still be wonderful, full of purpose and meaning. You just aren't likely to be spending as much on expensive fun as you did when you first stepped out of the office. And those are the years when healthcare costs can get really scary, especially if they mean assisted living or a skilled nursing facility.

Now let's take a peek at those roadblocks that can slow your plan or derail it entirely.

# Headwind #1: Market Risk

"'Wall Street,' reads the sinister old gag, 'is a street with a river at one end and a graveyard at the other.' This is striking, but incomplete. It omits the kindergarten in the middle, and that's what this book is about."

Fred Schwed, *Where are the Customers' Yachts?*

If growing a nest egg was easy, everyone would do it! Unfortunately, you'll face several headwinds that make that task harder.

The first headwind is market volatility. Investing for the long run means buying stocks. Bonds and cash don't give you the return you need, particularly when it comes to outpacing inflation. We can look at historical results and say, "stocks have historically appreciated at about 10% per year." But we all know past performance is no guarantee of future returns, and stocks certainly don't go up 10% every year. From 1872 to 2022, the Standard & Poor's 500, a commonly followed index of 500 large U.S. stocks, went up in 69% of years. There were three years when it was up 40- 50%, and two years when it was up over 50%! But it also went down 31% of the time, with six years when it dropped from 20-30%, and five years when it dropped by more than 30%.

Market downturns can take years to recover. That's primarily due to math. If the market goes down 20% in one year, then back up 20% the next, you won't find yourself back where you started. That's because the 20% gain builds from a smaller base. Start with $100 and lose $20, and you'll be down to $80. Start with the same $80 and gain 20%, and you're back to just $96. It takes a 25% gain to restore a 20% loss. It takes a 100% gain to restore a 50% loss!

### S&P 500 By Year

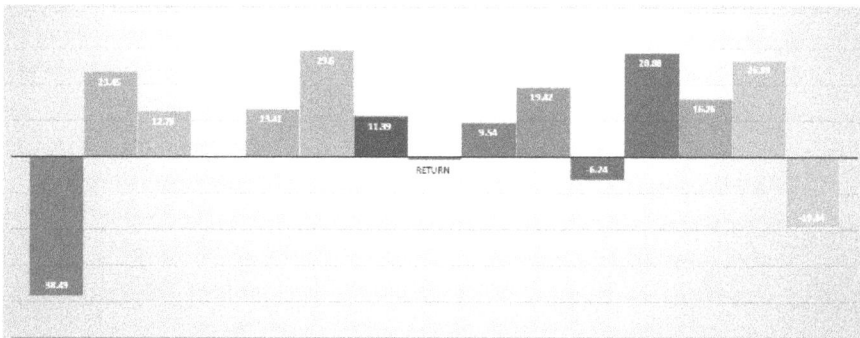

That sort of volatility is hard to stomach. Yes, stocks have always recovered over time. The market has never declined over any 20-year period (20 years!). But that's cold comfort when you're driving home from a long day—the kind that makes you want to retire right now, thank you very much—and you hear on the radio that the Dow dropped 5% or 6% that day. Maybe you go online to check your 401(k) and see a year's worth of savings less than you had a month ago, a week ago, or a day ago. People are only human, and emotion trumps reason. (There's an entire academic discipline, called behavioral finance, that studies why investors, as a group, are such boneheads. It's fascinating stuff, and several economists have won Nobel prizes trying to understand and explain it.) Are you truly confident you have the discipline to "just ride it out"? Research shows us that most investors don't.

Dalbar, Inc. is the country's leading financial services market research firm. Every year they study how average investors fare relative to overall markets. They report that for the 30-year period from January 1, 1992, to December 31, 2021, the S&P 500 went up an average of 10.1% per year. That's great! $100,000 turns into $2,082,296! But the average retail investor earned just 7.1% during that same period, meaning that same $100,000 turned into just $789,465.

Why do average investors do so much worse than the unmanaged indexes? Mostly, it's because they buy and sell at the wrong time. They try to time the market. They hear their favorite newscaster discussing signs of a market top, or predicting a recession, and they decide to sell their stocks, ride out the storm in cash, and get back in before the next big upswing. (Isn't that what CNBC is for?) Or they white-knuckle it for six months or a year while the market slides and throw in the towel right before the bottom. Either way, they miss the turn at the bottom and don't get back in until they're convinced it's "real"—six months later. By then, it's too late.

Seriously. When stocks recover, they usually do it fast. If you're out of the market when the rebound comes, you'll miss those gains forever. And just a few days can make all the difference in the world.

Let's say that on January 1, 2002, you invested $10,000 in the S&P 500. If you stayed invested for

20 years, you would have finished that period with $61,685. But if you had missed the market's ten best days during that time, you would have cut your return to just $28,260. Missing just ten days costs you nearly 65% of the market's gain!

Trying to beat the market is tempting! But doing it consistently without taking unnecessary risks is nearly impossible. The cleverest people on Wall Street spend millions of hours and billions of dollars trying to squeeze out an extra percent or two of "alpha," or above-market return. And they routinely blow themselves up trying. In 1998, a hedge fund called Long-Term Capital Management, with two Nobel Prize winners helping guide them, lost $4.6 billion in less than four months and needed a $3.6 billion bailout from the Federal Reserve to avoid taking the rest of the market down with them. In 2006, traders at Bear Stearns, Inc. lost $1.6 billion betting on subprime mortgages before the Fed stepped in to engineer a fire sale. In 2021, a former hedge fund manager named Bill Hwang lost $20 billion in his family office in just two days.

In the end, most investors aren't nearly as interested in beating the market when it's going up as they are in covering their backside when it goes down. That's where investment plans fall apart! So, they engage in a process called "asset allocation." Instead of just investing 100% of their assets in stocks and crossing their fingers, they spread their stocks out in different classes (large cap versus small cap, value versus growth, domestic versus international). They put part of their portfolio in less-volatile bonds and another part in risk-free cash. When large-cap value zigs, small-cap growth will zag. When stocks are down, bonds may be up. It's nothing more than your Depression-era grandmother's advice not to put all your eggs in one basket.

The problem with mixing bonds and cash into your portfolio is that they historically return less over time. They slow down the process of reaching that magic "number" that lets you retire. That makes the asset allocation process a series of tradeoffs—how much return are you willing to give up in exchange for security? Investment professionals have all sorts of rules of thumb for deciding how much to put where. "Subtract your age from 100%; that's how much of your portfolio you should keep in stocks," is one standard recommendation. Other advisors swear by the classic

60/40 portfolio, with 60% in stocks and 40% in bonds.

Asset allocation can help temper the stock market's volatility. But even diversified portfolios can fall when asset classes fall together. In 2022, a 60/40 portfolio lost 18.1%—the second-worst year (behind the "Great Recession" of 2008) since the inception of the Bloomberg US Aggregate Bond Index in 1976. Sometimes everything zags at once!

Make no mistake here. When it comes to managing your money, you're on your own, especially in the accumulation phase of the process. Few financial advisors are interested in working with 401(k) investors. They'll be happy to take your rollover when you retire, usually for a fee of 1% of assets under management. But until then, good luck!

Some plan sponsors offer "target date" funds, tied to your retirement date, to manage those risks for you. For example, if you plan to retire in 2040, you can invest now in a fund designed to gradually lower your equity exposure, and thus your volatility, as you get closer to that target date. Target date fund sponsors argue this helps make investment decisions easier and stay disciplined. However, these funds can suffer from a one-size-fits-all approach, lack of diversification, and higher fees than other types of funds.

# Headwind #2: Tax Risk

The next headwind is taxes. That might surprise you, considering the whole point of a tax-deferred account is to save on taxes! But as their name implies, tax-deferred accounts aren't designed to save taxes—they're designed to defer them. At some point, the tax still comes due. Deferring the tax bill from the time you make your contribution until the time you pull it out lets you invest the amount you would have otherwise paid in tax. But it doesn't always mean paying less. In fact, in many cases it means paying more!

When Do You Pay?

The Seed?     The Growth?     The Harvest?

Let's back up a step and look at how taxes work on investments in general. We can look at the process of growing any investment as a life cycle, with three phases:

First, there's the seed: your initial investment in whichever asset or account you choose. Can you deduct that seed, like with a traditional 401(k)? Or do you have to use after-tax dollars, like with a Roth IRA or taxable brokerage account?

Next, there's the growth phase, as your investment grows (or shrinks) over time. Are you paying taxes on interest, dividends, rents, or royalties you earn? Or are you protecting them in an account where you don't have to pay? Obviously, you'll be able to compound your returns faster if Uncle Sam isn't reaching in every year to pull out taxes.

Finally, there's the harvest phase when you start pulling out cash. This can include harvesting the fruit in the form of interest or dividends. Or it can take the form of cutting down the tree, as when you sell an investment entirely.

Traditional 401(k)s let you deduct whatever amount you defer into your account from your regular income tax for that year. (There's no deduction for employment tax, which becomes an issue for high-income business owners.) That's a sweet deal! If you're in the 24% tax bracket, you'll save 24 cents in federal tax, plus whatever amount you would have paid to your state, for every dollar you defer into your plan. But that makes perfect sense, considering the whole objective is to boost your savings by letting you invest the whole dollar, not just the 76 cents you would have to invest if you were paying up-front tax on the dollar.

As for the growth phase, there's no tax on any interest or dividends you earn on investments inside the account. And there's no tax on the gains you earn when you sell investments inside the plan.

So far so good, right? Well, now we've reached the harvest phase when you're pulling money out. Now it's time to pay the piper. And you might be surprised to find just how expensive that piper can be!

## Income By Age

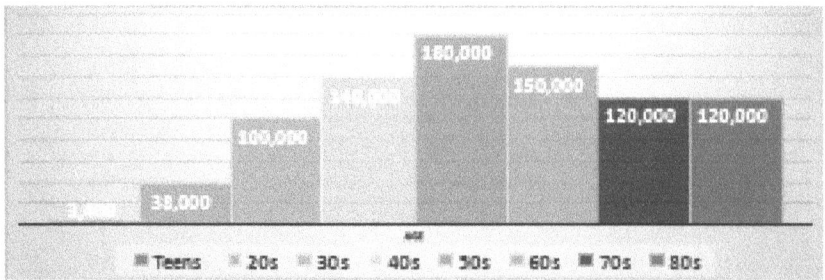

The traditional 401(k) model—using pretax dollars for money going in, and deferring tax until the money comes out—rests on several fundamental premises. The most important one assumes you'll be earning your highest income, and thus paying tax at your highest rates when you're stuffing money into your retirement mattress. It also assumes you'll be earning less and thus paying tax at a lower rate when you're pulling money out. What's more, it assumes that your relatively smaller contributions going in will be taxed at your top marginal rates, while your larger withdrawals coming out will get the benefit of moving up through the brackets before reaching your top marginal rate.

That may be true for most people. But it's not true for everyone. If you're just getting started in your career, your employer has probably bent over backwards to show off your shiny 401(k), including the value of tax-deferred compounding. But your new HR department doesn't offer tax planning, so they may not realize that you're earning less right now than you might in retirement. In that case, you may be better off passing up the current tax deduction they're dangling, choosing to defer after-tax dollars in a Roth alternative (which we'll discuss in a bit), and waiting until you're earning more to take advantage of the tax break. Of course, you'll want to take advantage of as much employer matching money as possible. That employer match can justify contributing today even if you're in a lower tax bracket than you'll be when you retire.

If you're a successful professional or business owner, earning a high-six-figure or even seven figure income, you may be building enough future income from various sources that you'll never fall out of the top tax bracket. If that's the case, you may not be doing yourself any favors by locking yourself into expensive annual funding requirements and employee contributions.

Tax Rates Over Time

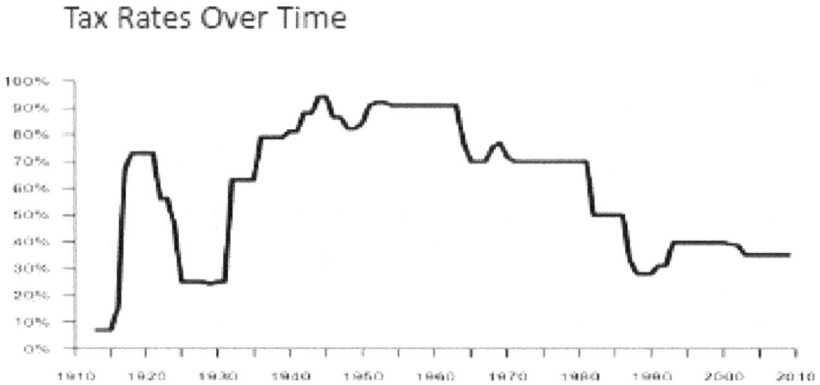

A second related question, which may be even harder to estimate, involves future tax rates. Your income could stay rock solid and steady from now until the day you die. But if overall tax rates go up, you could find a lifetime of diligent saving and careful money management turning into a tax time bomb.

While we can't know for sure what tomorrow's rates will be, we can draw some lessons from history. When Washington first authorized a tax on incomes in 1913, the top rate was just 7% on income over $10,000. Rates quickly climbed in World War I, fell back to the mid-20s in the Roaring Twenties, and jumped again in the Great Depression. The top rate reached 94% in 1944, after President Roosevelt declared that "in time of this grave national danger, when all excess income should go to win the war, no American citizen ought to have a net income, after he has paid his taxes, of more than $25,000 a year." It remained at 90% or above until 1963, when Washington dropped it to 70%. Washington dropped it again to 50% in 1981, and 28% in 1986.

Since then, the top rate has drifted back up to 39.6%, and currently stands at 37%. But merely glancing at the chart above shows us that as high as some think it is today, we're still near historic lows. And the current low rates we enjoy today are scheduled to expire at the end of 2025, making it even likelier that you wind up paying more tomorrow.

None of this tells us for sure where rates will be when you retire. But looking over the broad sweep of history suggests they're more likely to go up than down. Washington's addiction to red ink makes that outcome even more likely. Politicians running for reelection don't like to acknowledge this reality. But their refusal to acknowledge it doesn't make it go away.

This risk rises as your planning horizon lengthens: if you're 70 today, you'll probably feel more confident about your future rates than if you're 50. But sometimes we can anticipate changes years ahead of time. For example, the rate schedule established in the Tax Cuts and Jobs Act of 2017 expires at the end of 2025. If Washington doesn't act affirmatively to save that schedule, rates will go up automatically. How confident are you that we'll be able to afford them after we just put $8 trillion on the national credit card to cover pandemic-related recovery costs?

Even if statutory rates don't go up, effective rates will climb due to the way the IRS adjusts taxes for inflation. In 1985, Washington started indexing elements like standard deductions, personal exemptions, and tax brackets, so that rising inflation wouldn't push taxpayers into higher brackets. The IRS has traditionally used the Consumer Price Index, or CPI, to measure inflation. However, the Tax Cuts and Jobs Act of 2017 specified a different index, called the "chained" consumer price index. This index assumes that as prices go up, consumers react by choosing cheaper goods. For example, if the price of apples goes up, you probably won't stop eating them – but you might switch from Golden Delicious to Granny Smith. (If you're a millennial, substitute "avocado toast" for apples, and you'll get the point.) Chained CPI rises more slowly compared to the regular CPI. The nonpartisan Tax Policy Center estimates that changing to chained CPI will increase taxes for 30% of the taxpayers in the bottom quintile of the income distribution, 70% of the taxpayers in the next quintile, and nearly all of the taxpayers in the top 60% of income. Bottom line, switching to chained CPI will function like a small but noticeable annual, across-the-board tax hike.

So, that's the first tax danger you face using a 401(k) to fund your retirement. You might just be kicking your tax can down the road to a point when taxes are higher than they are today. And that danger grows greater the more time you have between now and then.

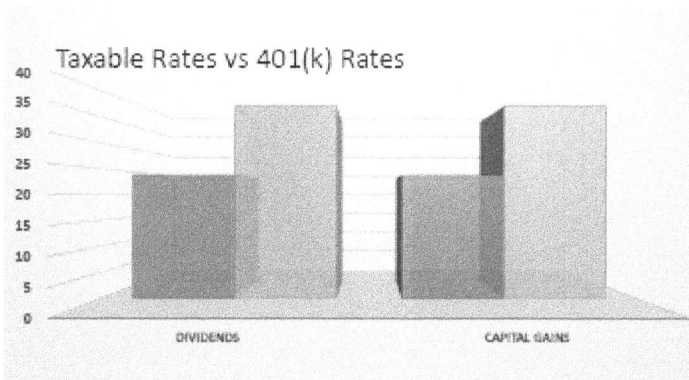

Taxable Rates vs 401(k) Rates

■ Taxable   Rates
■ 401(k) Rates

Had enough? Here's another tax danger with 401(k)s. You'll probably wind up paying higher tax on most of your withdrawals if you invest inside a 401(k) than if you had invested in a regular taxable account.

Most investors keep most of their 401(k) in stocks, especially as they work to grow assets before retiring. That's because stocks historically return more over time than bonds or cash, and you have more time to ride out the inevitable downturns while you're still growing your nest egg.

But stocks already give you built-in tax breaks that you lose when you buy them in a 401(k):

Tax on qualified corporate dividends you earn in a taxable account is capped at 20%, plus a 3.8% net investment income tax for taxpayers earning over $200,000 in adjusted gross income ($250,000 for joint filers).

Tax on long-term capital gains you earn in a taxable account is also capped at 20%, plus the 3.8% net investment income tax.

If you die while you own appreciated stock, your "basis" in that stock (the technical term for the purchase price used to calculate gain or loss) will be "stepped up" to fair market value as of the date of your death. That means nobody pays tax on any of those gains you earn before your death, and your beneficiaries inherit it with a clean slate as far as taxable gains are concerned. The Congressional Budget Office estimates that stepped-up basis rule will save Americans $110 billion in tax over the next decade.

There are several strategies you can use to avoid tax on stock gains entirely. For example, you can contribute appreciated stock to charity and deduct the full fair market value without paying tax on the gain. You can donate it to a charitable remainder trust or pooled income fund, sidestep tax on your gain, and draw income from the trust or the fund. You can sell stock, roll your gain into a Qualified Opportunity Fund, and defer the tax on that gain until 2026.

Finally, you can borrow against your stock for tax-free loan proceeds. Eventually, the amount of interest you pay on the loan will grow bigger than the amount of tax you would have paid on the sale. But guess what

. . . you still have the stock to keep going up! As long as the value of the stock increases by more than the interest you pay on the loan, you'll come out ahead. That can be a big "if," as we saw with the leveraged hedge funds blowing themselves up! But the wealthiest investors have used this strategy for years to live tax-free lives while their assets continue to accumulate. There's even a whole universe of "tax-engineered products" to help ensure the value of their stock so they don't have to worry if the value goes down while they've borrowed against it.

If you buy stock in a 401(k), though, you lose every one of those valuable tax breaks. Every single dollar you pull from your 401(k) gets taxed as ordinary income, no matter how you earned it inside the account. That means no lower rates for qualified corporate dividends, no lower rates for long-term capital gains, no stepped-up basis at death, and no tax-free loans.

# Headwind #3: Contribution Limits

**401(k) Contribution Limits (2023)**

| | |
|---|---|
| **$22,500** | Maximum Employee Elective Deferral |
| **$7,500** | Maximum Employee Catch-Up |
| **$66,000** | Combined Employee + Employer Contribution |

Here's another headwind to consider, although it's something many people would dismiss as a "champagne problem." If you're earning a significant current income and you want to keep that income through retirement, your 401(k) probably won't let you contribute enough to replace what you're taking home now.

For 2023, the current 401(k) deferral limit is $22,500 per year. If you're age 50 or older, you can make another $7,500 in "catch up" contributions. Your employer can kick in up to $43,500 more; however, the

49

average employer matches just 3.5% of your salary. $30,000 plus 3.5% of salary is a nice start. But will that be enough?

Let's say you're fortunate enough to be able to start maxing out your deferrals at age 30. You contribute $22,500 for 20 years and earn 9% per year, which is a tad higher than the historical rate of return for a traditional balanced portfolio (60% in equities and 40% in fixed income). At age 50, you bump your deferrals up to the full $30,000 per year and continue to earn 9%. At age 65, you'll have just under $5.1 million. Congratulations! Most people would call you rich.

But will $5 million be enough to maintain your lifestyle? If you start with the rule of thumb that you can spend 4% of your income, that will generate $200,000 per year. If you're used to earning $400,000, $500,000, or $600,000 per year, you'll be looking at some tough choices. If you're earning a million a year or more, you won't be ready to retire without significant cutbacks.

Now, we're not accounting for the employer match here. You might earn more in the market. You'll probably have at least something from Social Security.

But you probably won't be saving $22,500 at age 30, either, or even age 40. You might not want to wait to retire at 65. (And you probably aren't counting on Social Security. If it's there, great! But if not, you won't miss it.)

If you want to retire with $400,000 in income, you're going to need to save more than you can stuff into your 401(k). Where are you going to invest it?

# Headwind #4: Required Minimum Distributions

| Age | Period | Age | Period | Age | Period | Age | Period |
|-----|--------|-----|--------|-----|--------|-----|--------|
| 72 | 27.4 | 84 | 16.8 | 96 | 8.4 | 108 | 3.9 |
| 73 | 26.5 | 85 | 16.0 | 97 | 7.8 | 109 | 3.7 |
| 74 | 24.6 | 86 | 15.2 | 98 | 7.3 | 110 | 3.5 |
| 75 | 23.7 | 87 | 14.4 | 99 | 6.8 | 111 | 3.4 |
| 76 | 22.9 | 88 | 13.7 | 100 | 6.4 | 112 | 3.3 |
| 77 | 22.0 | 89 | 12.9 | 101 | 6.0 | 113 | 3.1 |
| 78 | 21.1 | 90 | 12.2 | 102 | 5.6 | 114 | 3.0 |
| 79 | 20.2 | 91 | 11.5 | 103 | 5.2 | 115 | 2.9 |
| 80 | 19.4 | 92 | 10.8 | 104 | 4.9 | 116 | 2.8 |
| 81 | 18.5 | 93 | 10.1 | 105 | 4.6 | 117 | 2.7 |

| Age | Period | Age | Period | Age | Period | Age | Period |
|-----|--------|-----|--------|-----|--------|-----|--------|
| 82 | 17.7 | 94 | 9.5 | 106 | 4.3 | 118 | 2.5 |
| 83 | 16.8 | 95 | 8.9 | 107 | 4.1 | 119 | 2.3 |

Here's another downside of investing in a 401(k). Washington created qualified plans to help you save for retirement, not create generational wealth. And at some point, they want the taxes they let you defer when you contributed to the plan. So, as you get older, you have to start withdrawing funds from your account, and pay tax on those withdrawals, whether you need the income or not. These are called Required Minimum Distributions, or RMDs.

To calculate your RMD, divide your account balance as of 12/31 (which your custodian reports to the IRS on Form 5498) and divide it by the period from the table above. For example, if you have $1,000,000 on 12/31 of the year you turn 80, you'll divide $1,000,000 by 19.4 to arrive at a $51,546 distribution. If you have more than one account, you can choose just one and take your overall required amount from that account, rather than making a series of individual withdrawals from each separate account.

For 2023, you have to take your first withdrawal by April 1 of the year after you turn 73. (Beginning in 2033, that age goes up to 75.) There are different rules for taking RMDs from accounts you inherit from a spouse, or someone other than your spouse.

If you miss a distribution, there's a penalty tax of 25% of what you should have taken. You can knock that penalty down to 10% if you take the distribution by the end of the second year following the year it was due. You can also use Form 5329 to show "reasonable cause" for not taking your distribution and ask for a waiver.

The goal here isn't to make you an expert in the rules governing RMDs. (They'll probably change before you retire, anyway!) I'm simply pointing out one additional headwind for 401(k) investors who may not need all the income they're required to pay tax on. I mentioned earlier that many experts recommend taking no more than 4% of your account balance to ensure you don't run out of money. The RMD rules force you to take more than 4% per year starting at age 74. Of course, you can reinvest any excess that you don't need. But you'll have less and less to reinvest every year as those required taxes take bigger and bigger bites out of your account.

# Headwind #5: Business Owners' Dilemma

If you own your own business, you've got an extra challenge when it comes to sponsoring a 401(k) or any other kind of defined contribution plan. That's because you don't get an employer matching or profit-sharing contribution on your deferrals. You pay it, out of your own pocket, for yourself (which is fine) and all your employees. "Top-heavy" rules may limit your own contributions unless you contribute certain minimums on behalf of your employees. (Your plan is top-heavy if you and your most highly-paid employees own more than 60% of the plan assets.) If your payroll is big enough that can easily eat up all the savings you get from your own deferrals, and more.

Let's say you're a decade out of dental school, and you open your own practice. Your staff includes an office manager, a receptionist, and two hygienists, earning $300,000, which puts you in the 32% federal tax bracket. And you're paying your staff an equal amount. You're not getting any younger, so you decide to open a 401(k). You can defer the maximum $22,500 without problem, saving you $7,200 in tax. Great! But if you stuff too much into the plan relative to your employees, you'll have to make at least some contribution for them, too. The cost of those contributions can quickly eat up your tax savings.

Now, you might think contributing a few thousand on behalf of your employees is no big deal. After all, those contributions are deductible, too! But think back to what we said earlier about when you take your tax savings with a qualified plan—either at the front end (as with a traditional plan) or the back end (as with a Roth). Remember that the trick is deciding where you'll save the most tax. And that depends on how much you save today versus how much you pay tomorrow.

Regardless of which bracket you're in now, every dollar you have to contribute on behalf of your employees effectively cuts your current savings. You may think, "I'm in the 32% tax bracket today, and I'm expecting to drop down to the 24% tax bracket when

I'm retired, so I'm still 8% ahead." But if you have to contribute just $1,500 on behalf of your employees, you'll cut today's savings to 27.47%. If your employee contribution grows to just $3,000, you'll cut today's effective savings to 22.93%. Now you're looking at that upside-down scenario where you'll pay more tomorrow than you'll save today. And you're converting your qualified corporate dividends and long-term capital gains into ordinary income. And you're giving up the prospect of a stepped-up basis at your death!

You can even run into the same dilemma without employees. Without getting into the gory details, which would probably bore you, making higher qualified plan contributions typically means paying higher employment tax. That extra employment tax drops your up-front savings to the point where you risk paying more whenever you pull money out.

You may not have a real choice about offering a plan or not. If you're hiring educated, in demand employees in a hot job market, they'll expect it. You'll have to offer one to compete. Your home state may even demand it. But the bottom line here is that business owners who do the math often find that maximizing qualified plan contributions for themselves actually cost them more over the long run. That means having to find somewhere else to save. Fortunately, I've got a solution, which I'll talk about shortly.

# Headwind #6: Losing Your Legacy

Most of us love our children and grandchildren very much. Most of us would like to leave our children and grandchildren more to remember us with than just some furniture and family photographs. Maybe you want to help your children put your grandchildren through college. Maybe you want to help your kids with their own retirement. Maybe you want to keep a beloved family vacation home in the family. You probably don't want to spoil them or make them rich. But you don't want to disinherit them, either.

If you're interested in leaving your family with a financial legacy, you should be aware 401(k)s are a terrible way to do it. Just awful. That's because your beneficiaries will owe tax on every dollar they withdraw from your plan. As we discussed in Headwind #2, they'll pay regular income rates on all your qualified corporate dividends and long term capital gains. And they'll get no stepped-up basis on any stock in your account.

What's worse, under current law, beneficiaries other than your spouse are required by law to empty your account within 10 years of your death. If your children are successful themselves, in their prime earning years, that could mean they pay far higher taxes on those withdrawals than you would have paid yourself in your lower income retirement years. And taxable withdrawals can play havoc with their own tax plans, phasing out all sorts of deductions, credits, and other opportunities.

# Alternatives to The Plan

| 401(k) Alternatives | |
|---|---|
| | 🔍 Roth Accounts |
| | 🏠 Taxable Accounts |
| | 🏠 Real Estate |
| | ✓ Life Insurance |

So . . . 401(k) s are great. But. . . .

You might not get the investment results you need.

You might not get the tax savings you expect.

You might not get to stuff as much money into your plan as you'd like.

You might have to start distributions sooner than you like or take more than you need.

If you own your own business, the 401(k) might not get the job done at all.

Does that mean you shouldn't use one? Of course not. Especially if you're getting an employer match, you should contribute as much as it takes to get the maximum employer match. That's free money, and it's probably a mistake to pass that up.

Beyond that, though, the 401(k) gets a lot less valuable for a lot of people. Here are several alternatives when you don't have one, or it isn't the right choice, or it doesn't let you invest enough to reach your goals.

# Roth Accounts

If your biggest fear is tax rates going up, you can reverse the usual model to pay the tax now on the seed and avoid it entirely on the harvest.

Back in 1997, Washington created the Roth IRA, named for Delaware Senator Bill Roth, who spearheaded the legislation creating it. Investors loved the concept. However, there weren't many who could take advantage of it. The original Roth IRA contribution limit was $2,000. Eligibility is phased out for taxpayers earning over $110,000 ($160,000 for joint filers). You could convert a regular IRA to a Roth IRA by paying the tax on the entire account, but only if your adjusted gross income before the conversion was under $100,000.

Since then, Washington has greatly expanded the concept. Now the contribution limit has reached $6,500, with a $1,000 catch-up contribution for those over age 50. More importantly, you can treat your 401(k) contributions as Roth contributions, forego the usual up-front tax deduction, and withdraw those earnings tax-free.

There are also several strategies for making "back-door" Roth contributions, for example, allow you to contribute to a SEP-IRA or non-deductible IRA and immediately convert those funds to a Roth.

Finally, you can convert part or all of a traditional IRA to a Roth, no matter how high your income goes. However, this means paying tax immediately on whatever portion of your account you choose to convert. Unless you're already in the highest tax bracket, this can easily push you into a higher tax bracket today.

Choosing whether or not to convert your traditional IRA or tax-deferred account balance to a Roth is one of the most complicated financial choices you can make. And it rarely makes sense, unless for some reason your income is uncharacteristically low in the year when you choose to convert. (This might be the case if you're unemployed for part of a year or you have significant losses from a business startup.) Seriously, folks, don't try this yourself. Get professional help—it could save you from making the most expensive financial mistake of your life.

# Taxable Brokerage Accounts

One alternative or supplement to a 401(k) is to invest in a taxable brokerage account. Let's take a look at how the seed, harvest, and growth cycle plays out for different investments you might buy in a regular brokerage account.

## Cash

Cash equivalents anchor a portfolio, offer low but stable returns, and protect you from fluctuations in stock and bond markets. There's no deduction for moving cash into a taxable brokerage account or buying cash equivalents (money market funds). Interest income is taxable as ordinary income now when you earn it at your regular rate. It's also subject to the 3.8% net investment income tax for those with incomes above $200,000 ($250,000 for joint filers).

## Bonds

A bond is a negotiable promissory note that pays a stated interest for a stated time with a stated payoff. Investors generally buy bonds for steady income with potential capital gains. They also buy bonds to stabilize their portfolio and reduce overall volatility.

There's no deduction for buying bonds in a taxable account. But bond interest is subject to regular income tax and net investment income tax as soon as you earn it. Capital gains you earn from selling bonds at a profit are also subject to tax.

## Stocks

As we saw earlier, common stock offers tax advantages, relative to cash and bonds, even if you buy it in regular taxable accounts.

When you buy stock in a regular taxable brokerage account, you're using after-tax dollars. So, there's no break on the seed.

There's no current tax if your share price goes up. Cash dividends are taxed, but at preferential "qualified corporate dividend" rates. So, we'll say there's a partial tax advantage on the growth.

When you sell, you'll owe tax on that gain. But you won't owe the tax until then. If you hold longer than 12 months, you'll pay tax at lower capital gain rates. And if you hold stock until your death, your heirs get a "stepped-up basis" equal to the stock's fair market value at your death, which means they escape tax on the appreciation entirely. So, we'll say there's a partial tax advantage on the harvest.

Ultimately, investing in taxable accounts (other than actively managed mutual funds) sidesteps some of the tax problems you find with 401(k)s. However, they leave you vulnerable to the same investment volatility headwinds. In 2008, the S&P 500 was down 38.5%. Would that drop have been any easier to stomach in a taxable brokerage account than in a 401(k)?

## Mutual Funds

You need to be especially careful before you buy mutual funds in a taxable brokerage account. Mutual funds can help you diversify an investment in cases where you can't afford a portfolio of individual securities. However, their structure creates several tax inefficiencies that can weigh down performance in taxable accounts, especially as they compound over time:

Income dividends consist of income earned by the fund's portfolio – bond interest, stock dividends, etc.

These are taxable immediately, even when you choose to reinvest them back into the fund.

Capital gains dividends are profits from sales of fund assets. These are generally taxed as long term capital gains, regardless of how long you've owned your shares. These are also taxable immediately, even when you reinvest them back into the fund.

Capital gains dividends can force you to pay tax on gains that accumulate before you even buy into the fund.

**Example:** On January 1, the XYZ Growth Fund buys Snapchat at $40 per share. On July 1, you invest in the fund when Snapface trades at $60 per share. On December 1, the fund sells Snapface at $80. You'll get a capital gains distribution and owe tax on your share of the full Snapface gain, even though you personally benefit from just half of it.

Capital gains dividends can even force you to pay tax on losing positions. (In fact, they're the only investment that can force you to pay tax on losers.)

Example: On January 1, the XYZ Growth Fund buys Snapface at $40 per share. On July 1, you invest in the fund with Snapface trades at $80 per share. On December 1, the fund sells Snapface at $60. You'll get a capital gains distribution and owe tax on your share of the fund's $20 gain even though your piece of the fund actually lost that much.

Pay special attention to that last point because it's worth repeating. Mutual funds are the only investment that can force you to pay tax on losing positions. In fact, in the scenario above, you're paying tax on someone else's gain!

## Real Estate

Real estate has always been a popular choice for investors looking to build long-term wealth. Over the last 20 years, it's become more popular with speculators too. (Surely, those property flipper shows on HGTV have something to do with it.) Odds are good that some of the wealthiest people in your town are the ones who've owned property for the longest. Real estate as an asset has a high probability of appreciation and can  produce rental income or income from Deeds of Trust. And real estate is often said to be the most tax-advantaged investment:

First and foremost, you can depreciate the cost of your investment in your property over time, which means writing off the cost over a period intended to approximate its useful life. Land doesn't depreciate. However, residential structures depreciate over 27.5 years, and nonresidential structures depreciate over 39. So, let's say you buy an apartment building for $1.4 million. The appraiser assigns $300,000 of that value to the land and $1.1 million to the structure. You can deduct $40,000 per year even though you're not actually writing a check for that amount. This lets many owners earn a nice "positive cash flow" throughout the year while showing no income or even a loss for tax purposes.

If you hold property for more than a year, you can take advantage of lower long-term capital gain rates when you sell.

You can avoid tax on sales entirely by rolling the proceeds into replacement property. This is called a

1031 exchange. There are also alternative capital gains strategies our firm can offer that do not have the restraints of the 1031 and are more flexible than a 1031 exchange, such as the Delaware Statuary Trust, the Deferred Sales Trust or the Restricted Property Trust. These and other choices can have different capital gains depending on the client's circumstances and objectives.

If you own appreciated property at death, your basis in that property gets stepped up to fair market value as of the date of your death. That wipes out tax on any gains before your death and gives your beneficiaries a clean slate. (They'll also get to start depreciating it again based on that new fair market value!)

Sounds great, right? But is real estate really right for you?

Real estate is considered a "passive" investment, meaning it churns out returns year after year without your day-to-day involvement like an active business. But whoever first described real estate as "passive" obviously never managed property! Someone has to scout out properties to buy, which you generally can't do at your computer at 10:00 PM like you can with stocks or mutual funds. Someone has to list the property for rent and be there to show it to prospective renters. Someone has to take the 4:00 AM phone calls when the water heater bursts or the furnace dies. And someone has to spring into action when a tenant can't pay. You can pay a management company, typically 10% of gross revenue, to handle maintenance headaches. But those fees will eat into your overall return and can easily mean the difference between profit and loss. And we've learned since 2008 that sometimes property values go down as well as up.

Having said that, real estate is subject to special "passive loss" rules that may limit or even eliminate your deduction for losses. The general rule is that you can't deduct losses from passive activities, including real estate, against ordinary income from your salary or your business. You have to "suspend" them and carry them forward until a year when you show a taxable income from that activity or until you dispose of the activity in a fully taxable transaction (not a 1031 exchange).

There's a special "rental real estate loss allowance" that lets some investors avoid that general limit. However, that allowance starts phasing out as your adjusted gross income tops $100,000 and disappears entirely at $150,000. Thousands of high-income people buy real estate every year for tax benefits, then discover on April 15 that they can't take their paper losses against their regular income.

It's easy to see why real estate is attractive, especially if you aren't intimidated by the maintenance. However, if you're a busy professional, working 50- or 60-hour weeks while you're trying to raise a family and enjoy life, you might easily conclude that buying and managing real estate takes more work than you're willing or able to put in.

## Cash Value Life Insurance

Cash-value life insurance gives you several significant tax planning opportunities for supplemental retirement savings. If you've maxed out available retirement plan contributions, or deductible retirement accounts aren't appropriate for your circumstances, life insurance may offer a solution. Let's look at it through the "seed-growth-harvest" lens:

There's generally no deduction for premiums going into the policy.

Policy cash values grow tax-deferred. Gains aren't taxed unless you let the policy lapse and cash out for more than you paid in. In that case, your taxable gain equals whatever cash value you take out minus whatever premiums you paid.

Harvest time is when life insurance shines. You can harvest cash from your policy, tax-free, by withdrawing your original premiums and borrowing against remaining cash values. You'll pay (nondeductible) interest on the loan, but your cash value will continue to grow. Depending on the purpose of the loans, in some cases, the interest on the insurance policy loans may be deductible. Also, many insurers offer "wash loan" provisions with little or no out- of-pocket costs. But even if your loan interest accumulates, you're still generally better of than if you had paid tax on your withdrawals.

Pay close attention to that last point. You can buy a cash value life insurance policy at, say, age 40. Stuff

$20,000 per year into it for 25 years, for a total of $500,000 in premiums. Watch your cash value grow to $1 million or more. And take it all tax-free, in the form of loans or premium withdrawals. And, so long as you maintain the policy in force, you'll never pay a dime in tax on that "income."

Finally, life insurance cash values offer something stock markets can't offer—a guarantee. Depending on which type of policy you buy, the insurance company assumes all the risk of investing your cash value and guarantees specific amounts at specific points, like retirement.

Together, those tax advantages and investment guarantees make life insurance retirement plans an amazing 401(k) supplement. In fact, it's so powerful that I've dubbed it the "Beyond 401(k)" solution.

# The "Beyond 401(k)" Solution

Enough about problems. Let's talk about a solution! But before we explain why cash-value life insurance can be such a powerful retirement planning tool, let's take a step back and outline what it is, why it works, and why it gets such generous tax treatment.

Fundamentally, life insurance is designed to protect your heirs from the risk of you dying too soon. Unfortunately, there's a challenge involved in meeting that goal. It has nothing to do with taxes. It's all about how likely you are to die. It just makes sense that as you get older, dying gets more likely. That means that when you go to buy insurance for that risk, it gets more and more expensive every year.

## Annual Renewable Term Life

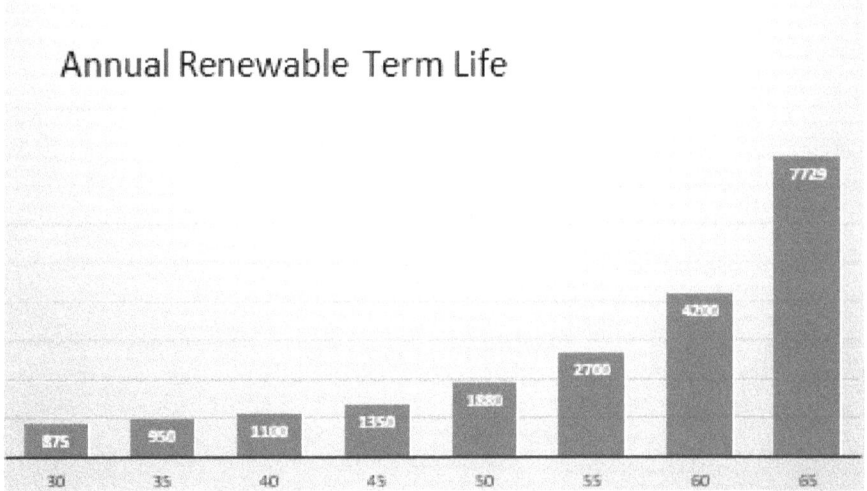

The chart above shows one company's estimated premium for $1,000,000 worth of "annual renewable term" coverage (ART), at varying ages, for a healthy nonsmoking male. ART is generally the cheapest coverage you can buy. It's priced for a single year, and "resets" every year going forward. As you can see, the coverage starts pretty cheap, at $875 per year at age 30. It rises slowly through the next couple of decades to $1,880 at age 50. But once the doctors start recommending colonoscopies and AARP invites you to join, things get pricey, with coverage rising to a whopping $7,729 by age 65. That's almost ten times the premium for a younger man.

If you don't die before your coverage ends, you don't get anything back. Now, for most insurance buyers, that's fine. You don't get anything back on your car insurance if you don't crash your car. You don't get anything back on your homeowner's insurance if your house doesn't burn down.

But for some buyers, term life is a waste. After all, we don't know if your car is going to crash. It probably won't. We don't know if your house is going to burn down. That hardly ever happens. But like it or not, we do know you're going to die. Someday. Hopefully in your sleep, after a life well lived. But it's going to happen. You can't escape it.

Insurance companies have come up with several solutions to make term life insurance more affordable. "Annual level term" lets you lock in an annual premium for a period of 10, 20, or even 30 years. The insurance company charges you more than you might pay for the early years in exchange for letting you pay less in the later years. And if you drop out early, that's fine with them, because they've gotten their higher premium early. In fact, they already know most buyers will drop out early, so they might even be able to price their level term less than their ART.

But what if you want permanent coverage? What if you want insurance to guarantee an estate for your heirs? What if you're a business owner, and you need coverage for a buy sell- agreement? What if you just aren't comfortable knowing how much you'll need 20 or 30 years down the road?

That's where permanent life insurance comes in. Permanent insurance lets you keep your coverage for as long as you live, so long as you pay enough into the policy. Part of each payment goes towards paying the cost of your death benefit. The rest goes into your cash value. As you pay more into the policy, that cash value grows bigger and bigger. Ideally, at some point, the income from that cash value grows big enough to pay for the cost of the death benefit all by itself. At that point, the policy is considered "paid up," and you can stop paying in.

Naturally, permanent insurance premiums are more expensive than term. That's because you're paying the cost of today's death benefit, plus extra to fund the cash value.

That's where the tax code steps in, shielding your cash value growth from tax in order to make life insurance easier to afford.

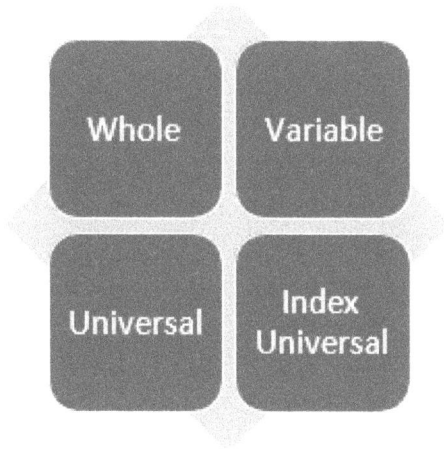

That cash value goes into a part of the life insurance policy that grows over time. Where does that cash value go? That's up to you. Insurance companies offer four main types of cash-value choices for different investors. The key is choosing a type that best matches your particular goals.

**Whole life** is the most traditional and conservative cash-value type, with required annual premiums and the strongest possible guarantees. This is old-school "big boy" life insurance. Policy cash values resemble a bank CD in a tax-advantaged wrapper.

**Universal life** resembles a short-term bond fund in a tax-advantaged wrapper. Plus, you can adjust premiums up or down so long as you pay the minimum amount necessary to keep your coverage in force. However, the policy cash values aren't guaranteed the same way they are with whole life.

**Variable life** segregates your cash value in your own account, separate from the insurer's general reserves. You can allocate that cash value among a series of "subaccounts" resembling mutual funds, with both the gains and losses of a typical mutual fund in a tax-deferred wrapper. Most variable contracts are structured as "variable universal life" (VUL) with flexible premiums but less strong guarantees. Typically, variable life policies offer two or three dozen subaccounts. These include a "guaranteed" account (invested in the insurance company's own general fund), a money market fund, a series of short-term to long-term bond funds, and a variety of stock funds running the gamut from value to growth, small-cap to large-cap, and international.

Finally, index universal life (IUL) policies invest most of your cash value in the same account they use for more traditional universal life policies to guarantee a minimum floor return, then invest the difference in an equity-based index. This gives you the potential for higher gains based on how the underlying index performs. When the index goes up, you get part (but generally not all) of the upside – and when it goes down, you get the guaranteed floor rate. In short: heads you win, tails you don't lose.

Whole life and universal life both have appropriate roles in the insurance marketplace. But stocks are the only way most investors will get the growth they need to replace their working income. And IUL is the only form of cash-value insurance that gives you that growth without the risk of losses you face with variable life. That's why we focus on IUL as the best available 401(k) supplement for the most diverse group of investors.

## How IUL Works

At first glance, buying an investment that gives stock market returns when it goes up, but protects you from losses when it goes down, sounds like finding a unicorn. Where do you find such a mythical creature? Aren't "risk" and "reward" opposite sides of the same coin? Isn't everyone on Wall Street working full-time trying to square that circle?

In truth, creating that sort of investment is easier than you think, especially if you're willing to give up some of the upside to buy protection against the downside. The answer comes down to a 200-year-old product called "options." Most investors who want stock market returns do it simply by buying stock. When markets go up, they get the gains; when markets go down, they take the losses. Easy peasy! The problem, of course, is that you can't know before you buy whether your stock is going to go up or down. But hey, markets have historically gone up over time, so as long as you can ride out the downturns, you'll be fine.

But what if you don't want to ride out the losses? What if you want only the gains? What if you want to read tomorrow's Wall Street Journal today? One way to do that, at least on a limited scale, is by buying an option. An option, as its name suggests, gives you the option but not the obligation to buy a stock after you've seen whether it goes up or down.

**Example:** Snapface stock is trading at $66 per share. You think it's going to go up . . . way up. But you know it could fall, too, and you don't want to own it if that happens. So, you go to your broker and buy an option. For $4, you'll be able to buy it for $70 at any time in the next 90 days. If Snapface stock goes to $75, you'll "exercise your option," buy it for $70, and you'll be $1 ahead (after the $4 option and the $70 share). If the stock goes to $80, you'll buy it for the same $70 and be $6 ahead. If it goes to $85, you'll buy it for $70 and be $11 ahead. But if the stock falls to $60, you'll let your option expire worthless and avoid the $6 loss you would have taken if you had bought the stock outright. For $4, you can get all the upside above a certain point, without risking more than your original $4.

You can buy options on individual stocks. You can also buy options on entire indexes, like the S&P 500. That's how insurance companies give you the same sort of upside in an IUL policy. They buy options on an index to give you the upside without exposing you to the risk of owning the index directly. Here's a 30,000-foot look at how it works.

# How IUL Works

| Premium |
|---|

| Death Benefit |
|---|

| Guaranteed Fund | Option |
|---|---|

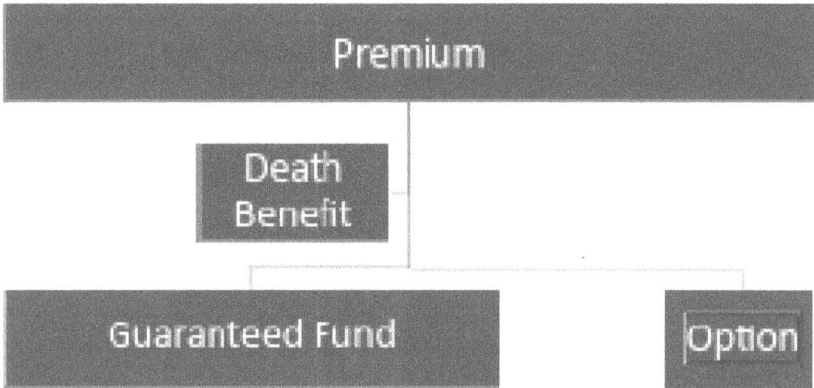

You pay your premium to the Beyond 401(K) Life Insurance Company.

The insurance company deducts the cost of insurance from that premium. Remember, this is roughly what you would have paid for an equivalent amount of term insurance.

Beyond takes most of your remaining premium and invests it in their guaranteed fund.

Beyond takes the last piece of your premium and buys an option on whatever index you've selected.

At the end of the year, the cash value invested in the guaranteed fund grows to whatever amount beyond the promised guarantee.

If the index goes up, beyond credits your cash value with the extra growth. Congratulations— heads, you win!

If the index stays flat or goes down, you still get your guaranteed return. You've avoided the losses you would have taken if you had invested directly in the index itself. Congratulations—tails, you don't lose!

That's really most of it. The rest is just details. Of course, different companies take all sorts of different approaches to the details. So, while IUL is straightforward in theory, it can get awfully complicated in practice. Here are some of the issues to look for in the fine print.

## The Index

The most obvious choice you'll make is which equity index you'll choose to determine your returns. Most IUL buyers choose the S&P 500 price index, which tracks the 500 largest companies in the U.S. by market capitalization. It moves up and down with the price of those stocks but doesn't include dividends those 500 companies pay. Investors like it because it gives them broad diversification across industry sectors and covers 70-80% of the entire U.S. market's value. However, IUL providers offer a variety of different indexes, including the Dow Jones Industrial Average, the NASDAQ 100, and even some international indexes.

## Crediting Method

The "crediting method" tells you exactly how the insurance company credits the index's gains to your policy.

**"Point-to-point" crediting** looks at the value of the index at two different points in time—typically the beginning and the end of the year—and credits you with the difference up to your policy's stated crediting cap.

**Example:** On January 1, 2024, the S&P 500 stands at 4,000 points, and your cash value at $100,000. On December 31, the index finishes at 5,000 points, for a 25% gain. Your contract gives you 100% of the index gain up to 12%, meaning your cash value grows by 12% of $100,000, or $12,000.

**"Monthly sum crediting"** looks at the index's percentage rise or fall each month and adds them up.

If the overall percentage for the year is a gain, you'll get that amount—again, up to your policy's stated cap.

Finally, "monthly average crediting" looks at the value of your index at the end of every month and averages them. If the final result is a gain, it gets credited to your account (up to the cap).

## Participation Rate

The participation rate tells you how much of the index's gain you get. Typically, this is 100%, meaning that if the index goes up by 10%, you get 100% of that gain or 10%. However, some "Hi- Par" (high participation) policies give you over 100% of the index's gain. For example, you might get "150% of the index's return up to 10%," meaning that if the index rises 10% in a year, your cash value will go up 15%.

## Threshold Rate

Some policies impose a threshold rate that the index has to clear before the carrier credits your account. If the threshold rate is, say, 5%, and the index goes up 15%, you'll be credited 10% in your account.

## Cap Rate

The "cap rate" limits how much your policy cash value can grow in a particular year. Cap rates typically aren't fixed for the life of your policy— they rise and fall with interest rates. That's because when prevailing interest rates are lower, insurance companies have less money to buy the options they use to capture the index's growth.

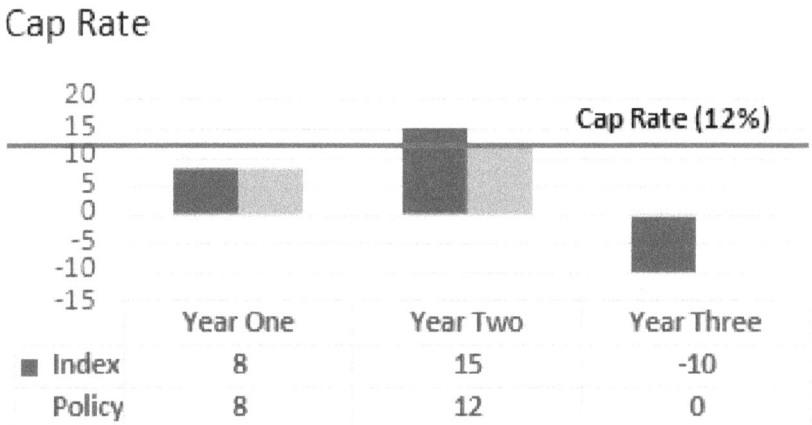

Cap Rate

| | Year One | Year Two | Year Three |
|---|---|---|---|
| Index | 8 | 15 | -10 |
| Policy | 8 | 12 | 0 |

Cap Rate (12%)

**Example:** You buy an IUL policy with a 12% cap rate. In Year One, the index goes up 8%, so your policy credits you with 8% growth. In Year Two, the index goes up 15%, so your policy credits you with 12% growth. In Year Three, the index goes down 10%, so your policy credits you with zero growth.

Cap rates play a huge part in determining how well your policy performs over time. The chart below uses back testing to illustrate how IUL policies with different cap rates would have performed from 1995 through 2019. For that 25- year period, the S&P 500 gained 8.12% per year. For that same period, an S&P 500-linked IUL with a 14% cap would have returned 8.47%. A 12% cap would have produced a 7.56% return. A 10% cap would have lowered the return to 6.51%. An 8% cap would have returned 5.32%. And a 6% cap would have returned just 4.07%.

## Performance by Gains Cap

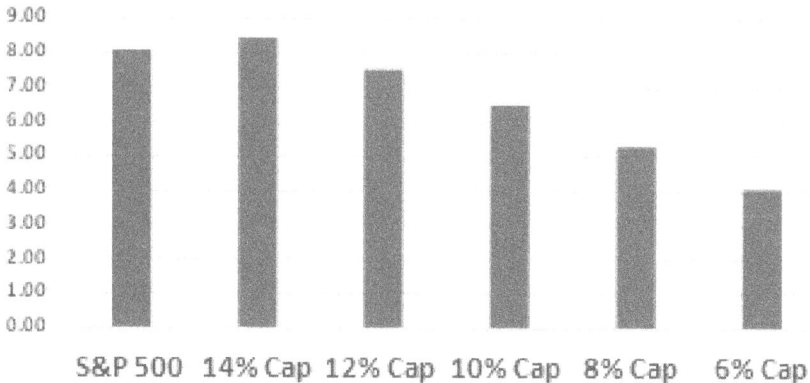

By now, you can see that IUL is complicated. It's not something you go online and buy like a mutual fund or term insurance. It's crucial to find an advisor who understands what you need to accomplish, who knows how to make all the moving parts work, and who can work with you over time to review your policy as markets move up and down. That's where I come in!

## How IUL Manages **Volatility**

It's easy to love stocks when they go up. But it's a lot harder to love them when they come back down, even when you know that historically they've gone up more than they've come down. As we've already seen, few investors have the patience and discipline to ride out those downswings. That's when they make the expensive decision to bail out. And that, in turn, costs them huge gains when the market rebounds.

IUL eliminates the stress you feel during a down market by eliminating those downturns. It also eliminates the time you have to spend recovering after the market drops. In 2000, 2001, and 2002, for example, the S&P 500 was down 9.10%, 11.89%, and 22.10%, respectively. In 2003, 2004, 2005, and 2006, it went back up by 28.68%, 10.88%, 4.91%, and 15.79%. If you had invested $1,000 directly in the index, it would have taken you until 2006 to get even. But if you had bought an IUL policy with a 12% growth cap, you would have started from even in 2003 and grown to $16,765 by the end of 2006.

At first glance, IUL looks like such a no- brainer that you might wonder why anyone would buy anything else. But remember, while you'll miss all of the index's downside, you'll also miss some of the upside, too. So, you'll miss big chunks of the gain in years like 2003 (up 26.86%), 2009 (up 26.46%), 2013 (up 32.39%), and 2017 (up 21.83%).

IUL isn't a free lunch. That shouldn't surprise you—nothing on Wall Street ever is. It's not designed to match whatever index your policy tracks. It's designed to use the index to beat the returns you would get in a whole life or universal life environment without exposing you to the risk you would assume in a variable life environment. That's why I recommend IUL as the ideal life insurance plan—because it gives you such a great combination of upside potential and downside protection, all wrapped up in a tax-advantaged bow. However, besides the tax advantages, the IUL must also be customized for individual goals and suitability. The IUL is neither good nor bad but is just an instrument that must be structured and customized for each individual client's goals and suitability. I remember a saying from my operating room days: successful surgery sometimes depends on who is holding the scalpel.

## How IUL Manages Taxes

When you sell investments within your 401(k), you don't pay tax on those gains. That's because you pay tax only when you pull cash from the account. As we saw in Chapter Two, all income is taxed at whatever ordinary rate you'll pay at the time you take it out. There is no potential to benefit from lower rates on qualified corporate dividends or long-term capital gains. And there's no potential to profit from a stepped-up basis at your death.

IUL avoids tax by letting you borrow from your policy. Loan proceeds are tax-free, so you can access as much as you want at whatever age you are without cutting the IRS in for a piece of your action. Here's how it works:

- You submit a loan request to Beyond Life Insurance for $10,000.

- Beyond Life takes $10,000 out of your cash value and moves it into an interest-bearing collateral account.

- Beyond then lends you the $10,000 out of its own pocket and charges your loan account interest.

As long as your policy qualifies as "insurance" under Code Section 7702—meaning, as long as you still have a single dollar of cash value—your entire outstanding loan balance remains tax-free. If the policy lapses, any loan balance greater than the amount of premium you've put into the policy becomes taxable as ordinary income. (Some policies offer an "over-loan protection rider" that steps in to reduce your death benefit and pay up the remainder of the policy.)

Obviously, the loan rate you pay is key. Ideally, the amount you earn in the loan collateral account and the amount you pay are the same, making the loan tax-free and cost-free. Some companies cap the loan rate, which is usually a significantly lower rate than a bank loan, and some companies guarantee the difference will never be more than a certain spread, such as 0.25%.

Some insurers offer a variable loan rate option. Typically, this means they'll credit your collateral account with the same performance as your cash value and charge your loan account a variable rate based on a different index, such as the old LIBOR. The Secured Overnight Financing Rate (SOFR) offcially replaced the LIBOR index on June 30, 2023. In the short run, that can be expensive—if your index goes down in any particular year, your loan balance will jump in the amount of interest you owe. Over time, though, the extra growth in the collateral account can mean significantly more cash to borrow in retirement.

As you borrow for retirement income, your cumulative loan balance will climb into hundreds of thousands of dollars. It may even top a million. Don't let the thought of "borrowing" that much intimidate you. Remember, the "loan" is really just an accounting device that protects your distributions from taxes. You should always be able to pay back your entire loan balance at any time.

While we're on the topic of taxes, here are two more reasons why IUL is such a valuable retirement income source:

Loan proceeds don't increase your "modified adjusted gross income" for purposes of taxing your Social Security benefits the way 401(k) withdrawals or taxable investment income do.

Loan proceeds aren't subject to the 3.8% "unearned income Medicare contribution" on investment income for those earning over $200,000 ($250,000 for joint filers).

However, whatever the insurance company loan rate, it is of course, a cost, but generally with a fixed Cap and, in most cases, less than current bank rates. Therefore, you also have an arbitrage in your favor as compared with paying the tax on a distribution from a taxable 401(k). In the next few paragraphs, I am going to emphasize some other important points to pay attention to and which are also discussed in more depth in other parts of this book.

The money you need now can be borrowed as a loan from your IUL policy for any personal purpose because you are using the cash value in your insurance policy as collateral. This cash value collateral is still in your policy is invested in the stock market for you and is still a working capital asset. This is very similar to a bank passbook loan, which also allows you to borrow against your own savings balance. However, loans from your 401(k) will reduce your 401(k) savings and will completely remove that amount of money from your 401(k) savings until paid back.

In many cases Rate of Return in an IUL can make more than what it takes to borrow from the policy as the policy has a fixed rate with a "cap rate". That loan from the policy is almost always lower that current bank rate loans. This of course depends on if the bank has some kind of promotional rate, and can also depend on the purpose of the borrowed funds. For instance, you may get a deduction of the interest for a policy loan if the policy loan is for an investment purpose such as purchasing commercial real estate.

The IUL is also less expensive over time as a non-qualified complementary or substituted plan, than the 401(k). The eventual accumulated cash value of the IUL when properly structured, can also over time beat the 401(k) employes plans that are also accumulating savings from salary contributions, even with the standard employer 401(k) salary matching contributions. This statement is also true for government employees. Every case is different, and we do the math for our clients, and calculate everything out for a comparison on a spread sheet, or with illustration scenarios to see what makes better sense.

If your 401(k) is in the stock market, the S&P 500, which is a good indicator of stock market performance, has an average range of 9% to 15% and has averaged overall about 12%. When adjusted for inflation, this overall average drops to about 8%, and capital gains and your tax bracket take another bite. Inflation reduces your standard of living if you are on a fixed income. Of course, being in the stock market, you get 100% of the upside and 100% of the downside. If you have mutual funds, you are being taxed even if you do not withdraw any profits and you can be absorbing other mutual funds owners' losses that bought the fund at a different price.

If the stock market takes a deep dive when you are in the last 10 years before your retirement date and the first 5 years of your retirement, you may not have enough time to accumulate enough money to prevent you from changing your lifestyle because of market events that are adverse. More safety for your retirement savings is especially important during these critical accumulation years.

Taxes and inflation are almost always the biggest expenses to future income from expenses from investments and qualified retirement plans. Stocks tend to be more volatile when inflation is elevated, and this is usually not a good thing for your retirement account. Remember 100% of the upside and 100% of the downside, and more often than not it will take more time to recover from larger losses.

For the average stock market investor, the consistency of a lack of volatility is the turtle that wins the longer-term race. Whatever the stock market does, it's hard to predict a cyclical deep dive, which could take years to recover, and you now have a "Negative Double Whammy" because the loss of that capital is also a lost opportunity cost, like that withdrawal from your 401(k).

However, remember one big difference is a structured product like the IUL guarantees that you can never lose your principal and will only participate in the stock market when the stock market goes up. When

I was trading as a professionally licensed trader and market maker, if the account I was trading could only participate in the stock market when it went up, then volatility could be very good for my trading account. Volatility is measured by the VIX Index.

People are also living longer, and it is no longer uncommon to live into your 90's. Because of this, more elderly retired people are running out of money because their 401(k) cannot keep up with this longevity. The IUL can be your hedge because you are not paying any tax on your loan distribution from your policy. Depending on your tax bracket, this could be an average of 30% - 40% or more.

This is a "Positive Double Whammy" as no money for that loan came out of your IUL cash value account and that cash value money is still working for you. The money you took out as a loan can also be used for other investments like real estate or Treasury Inflation Protected Securities (TIPS). Now you can have your money keep working for you in two places. This can reduce the risks of not having enough accumulated retirement money.

The IUL, can be structured for living benefits, gives you tax-free income, and you also have a legacy component for your family or a charity, with no Social Security consequences or Medicare surcharges for Medicare Part B and Part D premiums. Individuals with higher incomes qualify to pay a higher premium for Part B and Part D as Income-Related Monthly Adjustment Amounts (IRMA).

More Americans are also being penalized by the IRS for tapping their 401(k) for personal emergencies. Borrowing from your IUL insurance policy is a low-cost opportunity when you need money now for any purpose. The IUL is actually your own personal bank.

Depending on circumstances, you can decide to either pay any loan back or never pay the loan back, because with a carefully structured IUL policy for this purpose, the death benefit can, depending on the cash value, cover the cost of a policy loan for you. However, as we recommended elsewhere in this book, it is always better to pay the loan back so your policy cash value can maximize. If you are still working my recommendation, is you should be always contributing money on a regular basis to your IUL, either monthly or annually and continue saving with your IUL.

Every IUL case structured and managed differently. However, for many IUL owners, the cash value is significant enough after 3-5 years to allow you to stop paying the premium. If you choose to stop paying the premium, your IUL cash value will also have less eventual accumulation value. However, that 3–5 year timeframe really depends on what amount of premium you can afford to start with, and can even be after only 2 years, depending on how much cash value you start with or have accumulated. The more money that is retained as cash value in the IUL the more money you eventually will have for your retirement or for a supplement income. Remember the IUL is a structured product and just a tool. Your IUL insurance policy can be a very rewarding personally customized asset, and is a very flexible tool kit when structured correctly by a knowledgeable advisor. As I mentioned a few pages back, "sometimes how well the surgery comes out depends on whose hands are holding the scalpel."

## IUL Premiums Versus 401(k) **Contributions**

Qualified plan contributions are tied to specific legislative limits. Insurance premiums are tied to policy face values with no statutory limits. If your death benefit is large enough, you can stuff millions of dollars a year into your life insurance policy.

Of course, death benefits cost money. You don't want to waste money paying for more than you want or need. So, the trick here is to buy the least amount of death benefit necessary to support your desired contribution and "overfund" your policy, paying as much as you can as quickly as you can, if you want to primarily use your IUL for tax-free income loans as a living benefit for retirement.

Sadly, these advantages aren't entirely unlimited. In 1988, as universal life and variable life were becoming more popular, Congress grew concerned that taxpayers were buying life insurance as a tax shelter. So, they created a new rule: if you stuff too much cash into the policy in the first seven years, it's no longer considered "life insurance." It's considered an investment, called a "modified endowment contract." At that point, your cash value continues to grow tax-deferred, and your death benefit remains tax-free. However, any withdrawals you make during your lifetime will be taxed as ordinary income until you exhaust your "inside buildup"—the gain you make above and beyond your original premiums. If you're below age 59½, you'll pay an extra 10% penalty on top of your regular tax. This is sometimes called the "seven pay" limit because it's pegged at what it would take to pay for the policy in full in seven years.

I'm not going to bore you with the details of how to calculate the MEC limit because it would just give you a headache. (That's what actuaries and software are for.) However, in 2021, Congress finally recognized that prevailing interest rates had dropped since 1988, when they originally imposed the rule. So, as part of the Covid-19 relief bill, they dropped the interest rate assumptions the actuaries use to calculate this limit. Specifically, the guideline single premium rate dropped from 6% to 4%. And the guideline level premium rate dropped from 4% to 2%. That move effectively doubles the maximum contribution for every dollar of face value. And that, in turn, makes IUL an even more powerful tool for the right buyer.

## IUL and Required Minimum Distributions

Required minimum distributions? Ummm, nope.

## IUL for Business Owners

The IRS recognizes company owned life insurance (COLI) under Internal Revenue Code Section 162. IUL solves many of the biggest concerns that business owners face with qualified plans:

401(k) contributions limits mean that business owners who are enjoying a significant income from their business today are not able to put enough money into their 401(k) plan to replace a future value of their current income, to maintain at least an equivalent, or better lifestyle during their retirement years.

Owners generally can't make significant qualified plan contributions without sharing them with employees. While most owners genuinely want to do something for their long- term loyal staff, the cost of those employee contributions quickly drains the tax savings they get from their own contributions. This is especially true for higher-dollar defined benefit and cash-value plan options. IUL lets owners create a truly personal retirement plan and keep all the benefits for themselves and their families.

Owners who take themselves out of the qualified plan equation can usually cover their employees with a SIMPLE-IRA rather than a 401(k). These are easier and less expensive to administer and avoid the fiduciary liability that comes with offering a truly qualified plan.

There are no required minimum distributions to worry about for former owners who have sold their businesses and can draw all the income they need from those sale proceeds.

IUL also offers a powerful asset allocation advantage that you can't find in a 401(k). Many business owners have most of their net worth tied up in their business. They know they need to diversify their net worth but may want more growth than they would get in a more conservative fixed-income portfolio, whole life, or universal life. IUL lets them profit from equity index gains without exposing them to potential losses.

# More IUL Opportunities

So far, we've seen how IUL offers powerful retirement savings advantages for the right saver. But we're not finished! You can use IUL to help accomplish financial goals even if you never reach retirement yourself. You can use it for intermediate-term financial goals on the way to retirement. Some savers may be able to put IUL to work to catch up on savings even if they started decades later than they should have.

## The Death BeneXit

Remember back in Chapter One, when we summarized the entire retirement planning process in a single image? The very first question involved how many years you have to invest – to add new contributions to your portfolio and how many years you have for your returns to compound. The more years you can spend shoveling money into that compounding engine, the bigger your nest egg will grow.

What happens if you die or become disabled and aren't around to shovel more money into that machine? Whatever you've contributed up to that point will continue to grow, sure. But if your plan for you and your family is built around 30 years of contributions – and you're only around for 15 of them – your plan is going to fail.

Let's say you plan to invest $1,000 per month for 30 years and invest it at 8%. At the end of that time, you'll have $1,503,042. If you die after just 15 years, though, you'll have just $347,952. Now, if your survivor keeps earning 8%, it'll grow to $1,155,089. But that's still just 76.9% of your original plan. Your survivors would need to boost their investment earnings to 10.5% over those next 15 years to reach your original goal.

Life insurance eliminates that risk. Death benefits give you a built-in Plan B to complete your retirement savings plan for your spouse or partner, even if you're not around to complete it yourself. Even better, those benefits are free from income tax. (Death benefits are generally includible in your taxable estate. However, as of 2023, you and your spouse could each leave your heirs up to $12,920,000 before owing any tax.)

## Family Bank

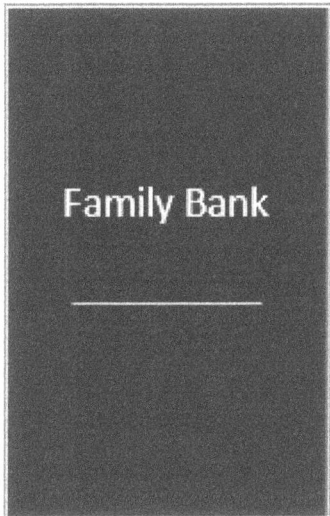

Saving for retirement probably isn't your only financial goal. You might also be paying down student loans, saving to buy a house, saving for your children's college, socking money away for a vacation home, and saving for all sorts of short- term goals, like a wedding, a vacation, or a new car. Juggling all those competing demands is hard, especially when the furnace at your rental property goes kaput, or your daughter announces her engagement. It's all too easy to put "saving for retirement" on the back burner. Or maybe you bite the bullet and borrow for those immediate expenses that just can't wait. Right now, Americans are carrying $1.6 trillion in student loan debt, $1.5 trillion in car debt, and close to $1 trillion more in credit cards. (If "faking it 'til you make it" were a state, its economy would be nearly the size of California's.)

You can certainly go to the bank, but borrowing money can be a pain. There's paperwork and red tape involved in convincing whoever you're borrowing from that you can pay them back.

Borrowing is also expensive. Let's say you find the SUV of your family's dreams for $50,000. You borrow $50,000 over 72 months at 6% interest. You'll pay $828.64 per month, which sounds reasonable enough. But at the end of the 72 months, you'll have paid $9,662.40 in interest. That money goes straight out of your pocket and into the bank.

Borrowing for a home is even more expensive, mostly because you're paying interest for a longer period. Let's say you borrow $800,000 at 6% interest to buy your home. The payment is a reasonable-sounding $4,796.40 per month. And your interest is tax-deductible. But by the time you finish paying that mortgage, you'll have paid $926,705.51 in interest. That's more than the amount you borrowed in the first place!

The same general costs (and hassles) apply whenever you borrow commercially, whether it's for business, investment, or personal use. Tax deductions are great—they help make borrowing more affordable, which is why the tax code offers those deductions in the first place. But in the end, you're still out the after-tax cost of whatever interest you pay.

In some cases, a 401(k) loan can let you borrow up to $50,000 or 50% of your vested account balance, whichever is less. This lets you pay yourself back and cuts out the bank. Here are the general rules and pitfalls:

You'll have to repay that loan, along with "reasonable" interest (typically a point or two over the prime rate) in "substantially equal" payments over no more than 5 years. (Some plans give you longer to repay if you secure the loan with your principal residence. That doesn't mean it's a good idea.)

You can generally have only one active loan at a time.

You'll lose whatever return you could have earned on that money if you had left it in your plan.

You'll repay your loan with after-tax dollars. Those dollars will all get taxed again when you pull them out in retirement.

If you don't repay any part of the loan, you'll owe regular tax on the shortfall plus a potential 10% penalty if you're under 59½.

If you're laid off or leave your job while you're repaying your loan, you may be forced to repay the entire outstanding balance immediately.

In some cases, a 401(k) loan might not be enough. You need more than $50,000 or 50% of your vested account balance. In those cases, a hardship withdrawal might work. Most 401(k)s also let you make hardship withdrawals for "immediate and heavy" financial needs.

These include:

- certain medical expenses,
- costs associated with buying a principal residence,
- tuition and related educational fees and expenses,
- payments necessary to prevent eviction from, or foreclosure on, a principal residence,
- burial or funeral expenses, and
- home repairs resulting from a federally declared disaster.

Different plans set out different rules for hardship withdrawals. But generally, you can take up to your entire vested account balance. You'll have to show your employer evidence to demonstrate your hardship (like a copy of the medical bill or eviction notice). You'll owe regular income tax on the withdrawal, plus that 10% penalty if you're below age 59½. And, of course, you'll lose whatever growth you would have gotten on that money if you hadn't had to swipe it from the plan. A hardship withdrawal can add years of work to your retirement plan.

The bottom line here is that you probably can reach into your 401(k) for money before retirement. However, that doesn't mean you should. Borrowing from your plan—or even worse, taking a hardship withdrawal—robs you of whatever growth you would have earned if you had left that money in your plan. That means a 401(k) loan can be the most expensive money you ever borrow. While plan loans and hardship withdrawals may look tempting, you should think of them only as last resorts.

Now let's look at what happens if you're supplementing (or replacing) your 401(k) with cash-value life insurance.

You can generally borrow up to 100% of your policy's cash value.

You don't have to give any explanation or provide any evidence why you need the money.

There's no application process or credit check. You won't ding your credit score when you borrow from your life insurance like you would if you were borrowing from a commercial lender. (Even just using your existing borrowing capability brings your score down. For example, if your credit card balance is more than 10% of your total available credit, you'll see your score drop.)

You won't owe tax on the loan amount so long as you maintain the policy in force. Even if your policy does lapse, much of what you take may be considered a tax-free withdrawal of basis.

You can take as long as you like to pay back your loan. You don't have to make ongoing payments (but as we'll discuss below, you should).

These advantages are so powerful that many advisors recommend using your life insurance as your primary lender. Why borrow from a commercial bank and pay them interest when you can use your own policy and keep the interest for yourself? The concept goes by several names: "family banking," "infinite banking," "becoming your own bank," "bank on yourself," "circle of wealth," or "perpetual wealth." All of them are based on the idea of accumulating cash value inside your life insurance and tapping it to avoid commercial banks.

There are two keys to making this strategy work:

First, you have to get as much money as possible into your policy before you can borrow anything out. That means overfunding it to quickly build cash value. (Notice how that coincides with overfunding a life insurance retirement plan to build cash value for retirement?)

Second, you should deal with your life insurance "bank" on the same terms as you would deal with a commercial bank. If the bank wants 8% over six years to finance your next SUV, then you should pay your insurance back the same 8% and do it for the same six years. You're not just cutting the bank out of the process of getting cash for your car. You're choosing to keep the bank's profit for yourself.

That second point may surprise you. Why pay interest at all if you have the cash to buy a car, business equipment, or a child's tuition? The reality is that you'll pay something for the use of the money no matter how you finance your purchase. If you borrow the bank's money, you'll call it "interest." If you spend your own cash, you'll call it "opportunity cost." But just because you never see whatever interest or growth you would have earned on it doesn't mean it didn't cost you. The real value of the family bank strategy is that you get to put the same money to work for yourself twice.

Remember, when you borrow against your IUL cash value, you're actually borrowing from the insurance company. The company takes the loan amount out of your cash value account and moves it into a loan collateral account, where you continue to earn a fixed or variable amount of interest. The company then lends you the money out of its own pocket and charges you fixed or variable interest. Preferably, those rates are the same, so the loan costs you nothing besides whatever greater amount you would have earned in the growth account. In some cases, with variable interest, you can earn even more than you pay. But if you pay "yourself" back at the same commercial rate you would otherwise pay the bank, you'll minimize that opportunity cost and come out even further ahead.

## Premium Financing

Sometimes you need more life insurance than you can comfortably afford. Maybe you didn't start saving for retirement until later in life, and you're looking at huge premium payments to catch up. If that's the case, something called "premium financing" may be the answer. At its heart, premium financing uses borrowed money to pay premiums. This lets you maximize your coverage and benefits without having to dip into your own pockets to pay for it all.

Premium financing doesn't give you "free" life insurance. You'll still have to pay a portion of the premium, or interest on the premium loan, out of pocket. But premium financing can leverage your existing assets to buy more coverage— including building more cash value. If you can earn more inside the policy than you pay to borrow the premium, you'll come out ahead.

Here's how it works:

You'll start by applying for life insurance and go through the usual underwriting process.

Once you have your quote for coverage, you'll apply for financing from a third-party lender— usually a private bank or life insurance lending company. Typically, this will be a variable rate loan for a specified period of years that you can roll over at expiration, providing your cash value grows large enough.

You'll have to pledge personal assets as collateral for the difference between the policy cash value and the outstanding loan amount.

Typically, you'll pay interest on the premium loan annually, either in advance or in arrears. The rationale here is to avoid compounding lifetime interest costs.

At some point down the road, either when the cash value grows large enough or at your death, you'll pay back the lender out of the policy itself. (Well, your estate will.)

Traditional premium financing is designed for high-net worth individuals and families— typically, those worth $5 million or more. However, there's a newer and significantly more accessible flavor of premium financing that offers similar benefits to less affuent buyers. The only requirements are that you be age 65 or under, make $100,000 or more per year, be under the age of 65, and be able to contribute at least $20,000 in actual premiums for years. This newer version involves no credit checks or loan documents, no interest payments, and no personal guarantees.

Premium financing may be an appropriate strategy if you hold mostly illiquid assets like real estate or a family business that you don't want to sell to free up cash for premiums. It may also be a great way to cover key-person insurance and buy- sell agreements.

## The 401(k)-to-IUL Conversion

Rolling your 401(k) into an IRA, and then converting that IRA to a Roth can be a great way to minimize future tax on your retirement savings. But most Roth investments leave you subject to the same stock market ups and downs that made saving for retirement so hard in the first place. What's worse, they do so at a time when it becomes even more important to manage your account to balance current income with long- term growth.

Unfortunately, you can't roll your 401(k) directly into an IUL. And you generally can't buy IUL in a 401(k) or IRA.

However, with a little bit of time on your side, you can roll money out of your IRA, pay tax on it the same as you would for any other withdrawal, and then contribute the after-tax proceeds to an IUL. If you do it carefully so that you don't push the tax on the withdrawals into a higher bracket, you'll minimize the tax hit. And you'll want to remember the "seven-pay" limit we discussed in the last chapter—you can't do it all at once (and still keep IUL's tax benefits) even if you want to.

You'll save thousands or even hundreds of thousands in future taxes. You'll add thousands to your after-tax retirement cash flow. And you'll eliminate the stress inducing market volatility that scares so many retirees into moving too much of their money into bonds and cash.

## The IUL-Financed Roth Conversion

Here's another strategy built around using IUL to convert your regular taxable 401(k) (or IRA) to a tax-free Roth. Remember, when you make that conversion, you have to pay the tax on the conversion amount. That leaves you with two tricky challenges, and you have to master them both to make the most of the conversion.

First, you have to calculate how much you can convert in any single year without pushing your income into a higher tax bracket than you would be paying if you were to leave it in the taxable account and pay tax in the usual manner down the road.

**Example:** You're in the 24% tax bracket today, and you expect to remain there in retirement. You can earn $50,000 more this year and stay in the 24% bracket. But if you convert any more today, you'll pay 32% on it. That's a bad deal because it means paying 8% more than if you had just left it in the taxable account.

Second, you have to figure out where to get the money to pay the tax. Yes, you can take it out of the converted account. But that means you lose the chance to keep growing that amount in a tax-free environment. Using an outside source of cash effectively turns that tax bill into a plan contribution.

**Example:** You decide to convert $100,000 of your 401(k) to a Roth, which you calculate will cost you $32,000 in tax. Before the conversion, your $100,000 was "worth" just $68,000. If you use $32,000 from the conversion account to pay the tax, you'll have the same $68,000 at the end that you started with. But if you pay the tax with outside dollars, now you'll go from $100,000 in taxable money to $100,000 in tax-free money.

If you've been raising a family and building a life, you may not have enough spare change in your couch cushions to cover the tax on your conversion. But if you've accumulated money in an IUL, you can take a tax-free loan to cover it!

At first glance, that may not look like an obvious benefit. You're essentially moving money out of one tax-free asset to convert a second asset from taxable to tax-free. However, converting your tax-deferred account to a Roth avoids all sorts of future costs. For starters, you'll eliminate tax on your future growth. You'll eliminate RMDs. And your future withdrawals won't count as "income" for purposes of subjecting your social security to tax.

What If Your Health Is Poor?

Throughout this book, we've assumed that you can get IUL at a decent price. And if your health is good, that's probably true. But what if it's not? Modern life is full of medical conditions that make life insurance expensive or impossible to buy: asthma, diabetes, high blood pressure, and any history of cancer, for example. Today's world is also full of behavioral temptations: smoking and drinking, scuba diving, and skydiving. If you're one of those hard-to-insure people, does that leave you out of luck?

Fortunately, the answer is no. You don't have to buy insurance on your own life to enjoy the tax and investment advantages of owning a policy. You can buy a policy insuring a spouse, a sibling, or even a child to give yourself the tax and investment advantages of owning IUL.

# Two Objections, Answered

Life insurance can be an amazing financial tool for the right buyer. But nobody wants it. They may need it, sure. But they rarely ever want it. Often, the reason comes down to a set of common objections that may or may not be true for you. So, let's take a look at two common objections and see if they hold water for your retirement plan.

## Should I "Buy Term and Invest the Difference"?

Some critics object that permanent life insurance costs too much. They'll tell you the insurance companies charge too much for administrative expenses and pay agents too much in commissions. They'll tell you to buy term insurance and take whatever extra you would have paid for permanent coverage, invest that difference yourself, and earn more than you would have inside a permanent life policy.

The critics are at least partly right. Permanent life insurance is expensive compared to term. But buying permanent life insurance doesn't make the death benefit coverage any more expensive. You'll pay essentially the same amount for your death benefit either way.

No, the old "buy term and invest the difference" advice is based on the belief that you can earn more in a traditional securities portfolio than you can in your life insurance cash value. And again, they were right, years ago, when permanent life meant old-school style whole life, which resembled old-school bank CDs in a tax-deferred wrapper.

But the whole point of today's IUL policies is to give you a guaranteed floor that "investing the difference" directly in equity markets can't, plus the chance to profit from equity growth. If you buy term, invest the difference in the stock market, and the market tanks, you're out of luck. The bottom line here is that comparing IUL with "buy term and investing the difference" isn't an apples-to-apples comparison.

And don't forget the tax advantages! You won't get those same advantages when you "buy term and invest the difference" unless you're investing "the difference" in a tax-free Roth account.

But the Commissions!

Now let's look at another argument against permanent life: the commission structure. Lots of financial "gurus," along with the writers at Money magazine, will tell you never to buy permanent life insurance because the commissions are so high. And once again, the critics are partly right—at least, the bare facts are true (if not the interpretation). But are life insurance commissions really that high compared to those you'd pay on other investment vehicles?

Permanent life commissions are typically 80- 100% of the "target premium." The Target premium equals the amount the insurance company estimates will be necessary to keep the policy in force for your entire life.

However, if you're using life insurance to create retirement income, you'll want to contribute more than whatever bare minimum you need to pay the policy in full. You'll "overfund" it. You may pay double or even triple that target amount. Commissions on those additional premium dollars typically range around 3%. That means, for example, if you pay double the target premium into an IUL contract, the commission will be more like 50% of your first year's contribution.

And then, the commission drops. That's because they're based on the first-year target premium. And in Year Two, Year Three, and beyond, there's generally no commission payable on that amount! (There may be a small commission payable on premiums you pay above target.)

If you were to invest that same premium amount with a financial advisor, you'd typically pay just 1% per year on that account. One percent is far less than 100% or even 50%, so the advisor must be a better deal, right? Well, not necessarily. That's because the advisor charges that same 1% every year on every dollar, over and over and over again.

Let's say you're comparing two investment alternatives. The first is an IUL contract with a $10,000 target premium and a $20,000 planned premium. The commission on that plan will be $10,000. Your second option is to contribute the same $20,000 per year to an investment advisor charging the typical 1% of assets under management. We'll assume the advisor bills quarterly. We'll assume the account earns 8.77% per year, which was the average return on a 60/40 balanced portfolio for the period 1926-2019. We'll assume you're doing it in a tax-free account, just to make the math easier. We'll even ignore the underlying cost of buying and selling individual securities or mutual fund management fees and costs. (You'll pay similar "platform fees" whether you're putting your money into life insurance or securities.)

| INVESTMENT MANAGEMENT FEE GROWTH | | | | | |
|---|---|---|---|---|---|
| Year | Starting Balance | Addition | End Balance | Annual Fee | Cum. Fee |
| 1 | 0 | 20,000 | 21,754.00 | 208.77 | 208.77 |
| 2 | 21,754.00 | 20,000 | 45,415.83 | 435.85 | 644.62 |
| 3 | 45,415.83 | 20,000 | 71,152.80 | 682.84 | 1327.46 |
| 4 | 71,152.80 | 20,000 | 99,146.90 | 951.50 | 2278.96 |
| 5 | 99,146.90 | 20,000 | 129,596.08 | 1,243.71 | 3522.67 |
| 6 | 129,596.08 | 20,000 | 162,715.66 | 1,561.56 | 5084.23 |
| 8 | 162,715.66 | 20,000 | 198,739.82 | 1,907.28 | 6991.51 |
| 9 | 198,739.82 | 20,000 | 237,923.30 | 2,283.32 | 9274.83 |
| 10 | 237,923.30 | 20,000 | 280,543.17 | 2,692.33 | 11967.16 |

In Year One, your advisor bills you $208.77. That represents 1% of the initial $20,000 deposit, plus 1% of the average balance of that 8.77% growth throughout the year.

In Year Two, your advisor bills you $435.85. That represents 1% on your original $20,000 deposit in Year One (which he already billed you for in Year One), plus 1% on the growth you earned in Year One (which he already billed you for in Year One), plus 1% on the $20,000 you deposited in Year Two, plus 1% on the average balance of that 8.77% growth in Year Two. So far, you've paid a total of $644.62 in fees, which is still way less than the $10,000 commission your insurance agent would have earned if you had chosen the IUL policy behind Door Number One.

In Year Three, your advisor bills you $682.84 in fees. That represents 1% on your original $20,000 deposit (which he already billed you for in Year One and Year Two), plus 1% on your growth in Year One (which he already billed you on in Year One and Year Two), plus 1% on your $20,000 deposit in Year Two (which he already billed you on in Year Two), plus 1% on your growth in Year Two (which he already billed you on in Year Two), plus 1% on your $20,000 deposit in Year Three, plus 1% on your growth in Year Three. But you've still paid just $1,327 in total, which still puts you way ahead of the commission your insurance agent would have earned.

Are you detecting a pattern yet? Every year, you pay the same 1% on money you've already paid fees on previously.

Skip ahead to Year Five. In Year Five, your advisor bills you $3,522.67 in fees. That represents 1% on your original $20,000 deposit (which he already billed you for in Year One, Year Two, Year Three, and Year Four), plus 1% on your growth in Year One (which he already billed you on in Year One, Year Two, Year Three, and Year Four), plus 1% on your $20,000 deposit in Year Two (which he already billed you on in Year Two, Year Three, and Year Four), plus 1% on your growth in Year Two (which he already billed you on in Year Two), Year Three, and Year Four, plus 1% on your $20,000 deposit in Year Three (which he already billed you on in Year Three and Year Four, plus 1% on your growth in Year Three (which he already billed you on in Year Three and Year Four), plus 1% on your $20,000 deposit in Year Four (which he already billed you on in Year Four), plus your growth in Year Four (which he already billed you on in Year Four), plus 1% on your $20,000 deposit in Year Five, plus 1% on your growth in Year Five. By then, you'll have paid $3,522.67 in fees.

By now the flaw in the 1% fee is obvious. You pay it every year on every dollar you invest and earn in your account. By year ten, you've paid 10% on that initial $20,000 deposit, plus 9% on your second $20,000 deposit, plus 8% on the one after that, and so on and so on. The same with all the growth you generate over those years. In fact, in year ten, you'll have paid more in management fees than the entire commission you would have paid on the IUL policy. In year 21 and beyond, you'll pay more than that commission every single year. Now how smart does it sound to "buy term and invest the difference"?

Those numbers are all hypothetical, of course. In reality, you probably won't earn that much after fees, especially if you're buying actively managed mutual funds. (The management fees and other costs that you'd pay on top of your advisor's 1% are such a drag that it's almost impossible to match the index.) And your returns certainly won't be so consistent. If you adjust them down, it will take longer for the cumulative asset management fees to top the one- time commission. But the basic premise still holds true. Paying a one-time commission on your target premium in the first year can leave you far better off than paying a traditional 1% advisor fee on your entire balance every year.

# Conclusion: Wrapping It All Up

So, ladies and gentlemen, what have we learned in the last couple of hours?

401(k) plans and other traditional (pre-tax) defined contribution retirement plans can be a terrific primary retirement strategy for millions of middle-income and upper-middle-income savers who can handle the stock market's ups and downs and expect to retire in a lower tax environment than the one they're paying in today.

401(k) plans can be a good first step towards retirement security for millions more, who will need to supplement their 401(k) with additional savings.

401(k) plans are a terrible strategy for millions of business owners, stock market skeptics, and anyone who's likely to be in a higher tax bracket tomorrow than they are today.

If you've worked your way through this book and realized you're in the first group, congratulations! Your time won't be wasted if you come away with more security in your future plans. And you'll have a better understanding of the overall "retirement industrial complex" so that you can pivot intelligently if your personal circumstances or tax laws change.

If you're in the second group, now you should have a better understanding of the gaps in your current plan. Your next step should be to call me to set up an appointment. We'll see if index universal life has a role to play in supplementing your 401(k) plan and filling the gap between what your 401(k) can accomplish and what you need to preserve your current lifestyle.

Finally, if you're in the third group, you should have a better understanding of the challenge you face. You should also set up an appointment with me, and we can discuss using IUL as a cornerstone and a basic, more secure foundation for your future retirement security that a 401(k) can't provide.

Financial happiness usually means having more money when you need it. At the very beginning of this book, Scott Peck, MD, advises taking "The Road Less Traveled." Take "The Road Less Traveled" and choose to have a more secure and wealthier and higher quality of life and lifestyle and less tax during your retirement, with a product very often used by estate planning and tax attorneys to help their clients succeed financially.

Will you have the will to go forward beyond the 401(k)?

To help emphasize the most essential take-action words in the previous sentence, please remember these two famous actors.

Will Rogers was famous during the 1920s and 1930s as a humorist and as an actor. Will Rogers, while probably wearing his cowboy hat and kicking back from the day, once said, "I am not so much concerned with the return on my money as getting the return of my money." Will Rogers might have rephrased his famous quote, if purchasing an IUL was possible during his lifetime. An IUL guarantees no loss of principal with a return on your money.

Will Smith, another famous actor decades later, also once said that becoming famous is amazing. But being famous is a mixed bag. And losing fame is miserable. It's not the actual fame that makes the difference in your life. It's the dopamine rush and the anticipation of getting, not the actual having, that makes a difference.

Thinking about retirement should give you a similar rush. Moving towards it and seeing yourself succeed at it should be amazing. Once you get there, it'll be a mixed bag. And if you lose it by running out of money, you'll be miserable. Go forward beyond the 401(k) and choose to keep the higher quality of life and lifestyle you deserve during your retirement. This book, along with my service, can make your anticipation a little more secure. You've already taken the first step by reading this far. Now take the second and let me help you put it into action!

# Questions and Notes

# Questions and Notes

# Questions and Notes

# Questions and Notes

www.ingramcontent.com/pod-product-compliance
Lightning Source LLC
Chambersburg PA
CBHW040900210326
41597CB00029B/4920